Rihanna
In Her Own Words

Rihanna
In Her Own Words

EDITED BY
**Kristina Dehlin
and John Crema**

A B2 BOOK

AGATE

CHICAGO

Printed in the United States of America

Library of Congress Cataloging-in-Publication Data

Names: Dehlin, Kristina, editor. | Crema, John, editor. Title: *Rihanna : in her own words* / edited by Kristina Dehlin and John Crema. Description: Chicago : B2 Books, 2023.

Identifiers: LCCN 2023007768 (print) | LCCN 2023007769 (ebook) | ISBN 9781572843257 (paperback) | ISBN 9781572848757 (ebook) Subjects: LCSH: Rihanna, 1988---Quotations. | Women singers--Quotations. | Businesswomen--Quotations. | Rihanna, 1988-Classification: LCC ML420.R434 A25 2023 (print) | LCC ML420.R434 (ebook) | DDC 782.42164092--dc23/eng/20230308 LC record available at https://lccn.loc.gov/2023007768 LC ebook record available at https://lccn.loc.gov/2023007769

First printed in July 2023

10 9 8 7 6 5 4 3 2 1   23 24 25 26 27

B2 Books is an imprint of Agate Publishing. Agate books are available in bulk at discount prices. For more information, visit agatepublishing.com.

Robyn is who I am. Rihanna—that's an idea of who I am.

—RIHANNA

Contents

Introduction 1

Part I: Robyn.. 6

Upbringing in Barbados..7

Love and Relationships 23

Part II: Rihanna... 42

Music..43

Fame 69

Personal Philosophy..85

Part III: Fenty 102

Beauty and Business..103

Fashion and Style 119

Philanthropy and Activism..137

Milestones 151

Acknowledgments 171

Introduction

Most Rihanna fans know a version of her history: "discovered" in Barbados, catapulted to pop stardom by Jay-Z, and abused by an intimate partner. There is also an essence of myth surrounding her today—though described by the media as being *always* late, when she finally arrives, people say that she is even more beautiful in person, glides instead of walks, and smells unreal. At the same time, she is known for her authenticity. Rihanna, meanwhile, says she doesn't think anyone truly *knows* her. What we do know is that she built a brand out of herself and claimed complete control over it.

Robyn Rihanna Fenty was born on February 20, 1988, in the Caribbean country of Barbados—a place she calls "paradise." She grew up there with two younger brothers and always wanted to be one of the boys. Even then, she was singing into her hairbrush.

But Robyn's childhood was also shaped by trauma. Her father was addicted to drugs and alcohol and physically abused her mother. Eventually, her parents divorced, and Robyn was effectively raised by a single mother. She was also inspired by another strong woman in her life: her grandmother.

Robyn always dreamed about being a singer, and at

age 15, she formed a singing trio with two friends. They scored an audition with Evan Rogers, a vacationing music producer. Rogers was wowed by Robyn and soon met with her and her mom to launch the young singer's career. At age 16, Robyn went to stay with Rogers and his wife in Connecticut. Within a year, she recorded the demo of "Pon de Replay"—the song that would later become her first hit under the stage name "Rihanna."

Rogers sent the song to several record labels, including Def Jam, where rapper and producer Jay-Z was president. Impressed, the executives at Def Jam invited her to audition. The audition proved so successful that Jay-Z and the others insisted on signing her immediately.

In 2005, Rihanna released her first album, *Music of the Sun*, with an island girl image and sound. Her second album in 2006 brought the hit song "SOS," proving that she wouldn't be a one-hit wonder. Rihanna found her true image and sound with her third album, *Good Girl Gone Bad*. Right before the album cover shoot, she dramatically chopped her hair, to the disapproval of her label. But the rebellious look and edgier sound worked. "Umbrella," the opening track, won Rihanna her first Grammy in 2008. From then on, Rihanna made her own artistic decisions.

As she took more risks musically and aesthetically, Rihanna faced backlash. She struggled with the pressure to be a role model. She posted photos to Instagram of her smoking weed, wore risky outfits, and played dark, intense characters in her music videos. These changes turned some fans and media against her.

In 2009, singer Chris Brown assaulted Rihanna following a Grammys pre-party. TMZ released photos of Rihanna's battered face and thrust her into the role of public victim. She faced constant, invasive questioning about the incident. Eventually, she spoke out about it in the name of helping other girls. When Rihanna later reconciled with Brown, she was met with intense criticism. She acknowledged that people would not understand her choices and decided to do what made her happy anyway.

Rihanna continued to release more studio albums. Her eighth album, *Anti*, from 2016, is often regarded as her best work. She has had a total of 14 number-one hits on the Billboard Hot 100 and has won nine of the 33 Grammy awards for which she was nominated. She has even found time to act in movies like *Battleship* and *Ocean's 8* and write music for the films *Home* and *Black Panther: Wakanda Forever*. All the while, she has built a massive and loyal fanbase (dubbed the "Navy").

She's also been busy with other endeavors. Like many celebrities, she released fragrances and partnered with beauty brands like MAC Cosmetics early in her career. But in 2017, she stepped into entrepreneurship with the launch of her own makeup brand. Fenty Beauty famously launched with 40 foundation shades and was quickly lauded for its unprecedented commitment to inclusivity, which has become the cornerstone of the brand. And this is not just another celebrity branding deal; Rihanna helps create products and gives personal makeup tutorials online.

The Fenty empire didn't stop there. In 2018, Rihanna launched Savage X Fenty, her lingerie brand. Rihanna is deeply ingrained in the business of Savage X Fenty, too. She approves the designs, models the pieces on social media, and produces celebrity-studded fashion shows. And like Fenty Beauty, Savage X Fenty is viewed as an industry disruptor for embracing diversity in its models and sizes offered. The success of Fenty Beauty and Savage X Fenty have helped her officially reach billionaire status, making her the richest female musician on the planet.

Rihanna is also known for using that money to help others. In 2012, she founded the Clara Lionel Foundation (CLF). CLF invests in education, healthcare, and disaster relief projects in the Caribbean and the U.S., with a focus on the climate crisis. For her philanthropy and activism, Rihanna has been honored with awards like the Harvard Humanitarian Award and was named a Barbados National Hero.

In 2022, Rihanna took on yet another new role: mom. She was very public with her revolutionary pregnancy looks of crop tops and jeweled chains, and she is open about her loving relationship with her baby's father, rapper A$AP Rocky. After her son was born, however, she kept that part of her life private. Then, she performed at the 2023 Super Bowl with a visible baby bump and confirmed shortly after that she was pregnant with her second child.

Today, Rihanna is charting her own path, on her own timeline. She chooses which parts of her life to share with the public. She runs her businesses with herself as the muse, and she takes as long as she needs to get her music right. She appears so authentically herself and so endlessly intriguing that her many fans are willing to wait as long as it takes to see what she does next.

Part I

ROBYN

Upbringing in Barbados

IN MY OWN household, my father is half black, half white. My mom is black from South America. I was seeing diversity. That's all I knew.

T Magazine, May 19, 2019

I CAN COOK, because I had to growing up. My mom is from Guyana and is a very good cook. I used to always be in the kitchen helping her out.

Seventeen, May 14, 2007

I'M THE OLDEST child with two brothers. We talk all the time now, but we used to fight—and when I say "fight," I don't mean arguments, I mean physically fight.

Complex, May 11, 2011

I ALWAYS WANTED to do what my brothers were doing. I always wanted to play the games they played and play rough and wear pants and go outside.

Vogue, April 1, 2016

MY PARENTS' DIVORCE was more of a relief
for me. Them being together—I love my dad, I
love my mom—for some reason when it came
together, it was always stressful. It was a lot
of pressure.

The Tyra Banks Show, October 26, 2007

DOMESTIC VIOLENCE IS not something that
people want anybody to know, so [my mom]
just would hide it in the house. I always said
to myself, I'm never gonna date somebody like
my dad. Never.

20/20, November 6, 2009

I SAW TOO much. I was way too mature for my
age. I guess that was why I became rebellious.
That's what my mother thinks anyway.

on her difficult home life, British *Vogue*,
November 1, 2011

I HAD TO be very, very strong because I had two younger brothers and I was like the protector. I didn't want them to see anything. And that really has a lot to do with the type of person that I am now, the type of woman that I've become, because I'm very strong and nothing really phases me.

on her parents' divorce, *The Tyra Banks Show*,
October 26, 2007

ONE OF MY best and worst qualities is masking everything. Whatever was happening at home, no one at school knew, no one would ever suspect. I didn't let it affect my schoolwork. It was always this feeling of responsibility—never letting it get past the house.

on her difficult home life as a child, *Vogue*, April 1, 2011

MY MOM WAS a single mom, so she worked a lot. She was really never home—I mean, she was home, but it would be after work, late at night, so I would take care of [my younger brother Rajad]. He was my best friend. He thought I was his mom!

The Guardian, **November 20, 2009**

MY MOM IS the one. She's like Superwoman, I swear. She's very forgiving but not a pushover in any way. Her energy is off the chain.

Vogue, **April 1, 2011**

A MILLION WORDS I can use to try to describe this courageous, fearless, selfless woman .... but at the end of the day no word makes her feel more special than MOM!!! How lucky am I to have come here through you? You nurtured and taught and cultured me...and then some things couldn't be taught, but were inevitable simply because I'm your daughter.

Instagram post, April 5, 2014

[MY DAD] TAUGHT me how to fish, how to swim, how to run, how to ride. He really toughened me up.

Rolling Stone, April 14, 2011

I ACTUALLY FEEL really bad for my father. He was abused too—he got beat up by his stepdad when he was young. He has resentment toward women, because he felt like his mom never protected him, and unfortunately, my mother was the victim of that. I'm not giving him excuses. Right is right and wrong is wrong. I still blame him. But I understand the source.

Rolling Stone, April 14, 2011

I WOULD SAY my relationship with my father has had a bigger impact on me than I knew. Even with the things that I love, the things that I am attracted to. A lot of it stems from the things that I've seen in my life as a child.

Glamour, August 1, 2011

[MY GRANDMOTHER] WAS a legend. She was a well-rounded woman. She taught me a lot about forgiveness. She taught me a lot about loving my enemies.

Oprah's Next Chapter, **August 20, 2012**

WHEN I THINK of my grandmother, I think of a very strong woman . . . very independent, but the most caring woman, very giving, very selfless. And all the women in my family strive to be like her.

"Rihanna's Clara Lionel Foundation," June 19, 2015

I REALLY HUGGED my cousin the night before he died; I didn't know why. Now each time I hug somebody lately, I hug them like it's the last time. That may be my biggest life lesson, not to wait on anything, not even tomorrow.

Vogue, **June 1, 2018**

WE DON'T START the trouble, but that's how
we're defending ourselves—by saying some slick
shit. That's how I've always been. I was so rude
when I was a little girl.

Complex, **January 14, 2013**

I WAS ONE of the boys. I never saw the need for
having girlfriends until I met Melissa. Melissa
taught me how to be a girl.

**on her best friend, Melissa Forde, British *Vogue*,
November 1, 2011**

WHEN I WAS fourteen and first started going out,
I always wanted to be the opposite of everyone
else. So I would go to the club in a polo T-shirt
and pants and sneakers and a hat on backward,
just so I would not be dressed like other girls.

Vogue, **April 1, 2011**

I WAS A bit of a loner at times. Cadets was my
one outlet. I didn't do any sports, I just did cadets.
Little things that you learn in cadets follow you
all through your life. Even the way I line my
toiletries from tallest to smallest. The discipline
really sticks with you.

W Magazine, **October 13, 2017**

GROWING UP IN Barbados, I did not always love
school. It can feel like a grind, especially when
you'd rather be singing, playing sports or doing
pretty much anything other than homework. I
realise now that I often took it for granted that I
was even able to go to school. Education can be
stolen from you in a second.

The Guardian, **September 18, 2018**

I GOT TEASED my entire school life. What they were picking on I don't even understand. It was my skin color. Then when I got older, it was about my breasts. But I'm not victimized—I'm grateful. I think those experiences were strategically put together by God for the preparation of being in the music industry.

Glamour, Septermber 30, 2013

A LOT OF the reason why I am the way that I am in my character has a lot to do with my culture, the way I was brought up, and the way we are with each other in Barbados.

DayBreak, March 29, 2012

PEOPLE FIND [MY performance] so sexual, but going back to Carnivale in Barbados . . . I really noticed that it's a cultural thing. It's the way we move.

Jonathan Ross Show, March 6, 2012

BARBADOS—THEY'VE BEEN VERY supportive, and I will always, always, always represent them, because even though I don't agree with everything they say, and I'm sure they don't agree with everything I say and do either, that's my home. It'll always be home.

Jonathan Ross Show, **March 6, 2012**

I STILL FEEL like I belong here [in Barbados], you know? All my friends are the people I grew up with.... They all still live out here. So, when I come I see a lot of familiar faces.

"Rihanna – Road to *Talk That Talk* (Part 2),"
April 24, 2012

#BARBADOS had been a British colony ever since 1627 when the British first settled there.... On NOVEMBER 30th In 1966 we achieved our INDEPENDENCE, and this day, every year we fly our flags highest!!! My country, my island, my people, our culture....Barbados will always be HOME!!!

Instagram post, November 30, 2013

Blessed to be from Paradise!!!

Instagram post, November 30, 2014

It's the way we are [in Barbados]. It's the way I've always remembered it being. People have always been hospitable and caring and welcoming—ever since I was a kid, ever since I remember.

"Rihanna Gears Up for the Second Annual Dimond Ball Benefitting the Clara Lionel Foundation," **December 7, 2015**

I basically grew up in paradise. I mean, people save for their whole lives to go on vacation there, and it's easy to take that for granted.

Vogue, June 1, 2018

WESTBURY is more than a community, we're family!!! Thank you for all that you've poured into my life and the woman I am! It takes a village, and I'm glad my village was you!!!!

on Westbury Road in Barbados being renamed
Rihanna Drive, Instagram post,
December 1, 2017

ANY CITIZEN OF Barbados, anyone who's been born or grew up in Barbados, for them to validate anything that I do, have done, or any representation that I've had of the country—it means so much.

fifth annual Diamond Ball red carpet,
September 12, 2019

WOKE UP FEELING like a Sunday in Barbados! If you know, then you know that's the best feeling in the world!

Twitter post, December 1, 2020

BARBADIANS ARE PROUD people, you know. We are probably the proudest people I know, and no matter where I go in the world, I take that pride with me.

Barbados National Hero acceptance speech at the National Independence Honours Ceremony, November 30, 2021

I'M SO PROUD to be a Bajan. I'm going to be a Bajan 'til the day I die. This is still the only place I've ever called home.

Barbados National Hero acceptance speech at the National Independence Honours Ceremony, November 30, 2021

WHAT AN ABSOLUTE honor to be amongst such great men and women who have come before me and held this title in committment to our nation!

on celebrating her first National Heroes Day as a National Hero of Barbados, Twitter post, April 28, 2022

I WILL FOREVER cherish these memories and continue to represent the Bajan people and my home Barbados to the fullest!!

on celebrating her first National Heroes Day as a National Hero of Barbados, Twitter post, April 28, 2022

MY FIRST TIME praying and fasting was when I was 7 years old. I did that on my own, because I wanted to go to New York, and I knew that this was a sacrifice I had to make in order for god to make sure I could get there.

Interview, June 10, 2019

THAT'S SOMETHING I don't think I could ever do. Send my only girl to another random country to live with people she'd just met. It had to be God that paralyzed Monica Fenty's emotions so that she'd say, 'Yes, go.' To this day, I don't know how that happened. But thank God it did.

T Magazine, October 12, 2015

ROBYN IS THE brick to my foundation. It's something I hold on to. It's everything I grew up with, my childhood, Barbados, people close to me. Everything that's familiar. People know Rihanna from my music. But if this were to all go away tomorrow, I would always look at myself as Robyn.

Rolling Stone, **April 14, 2011**

Love and

Relationships

FRIENDS ARE HONEST. And they tell you when it's good and they tell you when it's bad. And they're there for you when things are good and they're there for you when things are bad.

DayBreak, March 29, 2012

YOU KNOW IT was a good night when u wake up n run to your BFF's room like... How did I get in my bed? Did I walk? Stumble? Get carried?

Twitter post, May 20, 2012

[MELISSA FORDE] WAS my first real girlfriend and now she's almost always with me—we live together. . . . I feel like she's my guardian angel.

Seventeen, August 1, 2010

I SEE [MY staff] more than my family and spend
most of my life with them. It becomes friendship
first, and then it leads into family because we
lean on each other. I'm sure it's really different
from any other boss-employee relationship.

T Magazine, May 19, 2019

I'M ONLY AS good as my team.

**Icon Award acceptance speech at American
Music Awards, November 24, 2013**

I LOVE READING people. I really enjoy watching,
observing, and being able to figure out a person,
the reason they wore that dress, the reason they
smell the way they do.

Vogue, April 1, 2011

SPEND TIME WITH people who know how to
use their days well. Just as iron sharpens iron,
positive people will inspire you to be positive.

Twitter post, June 16, 2012

I'm very picky about friends. I don't like to open myself up to everyone and so when you find people who are great and loyal, you don't want to let go of that.

British *Vogue*, September 1, 2018

FIGURE OUT WHO knows u, who trusts u, who's important to u, whose opinions actually matter, and whose presence is irresistible.

Twitter post, September 9, 2012

I DON'T EVER want to have to depend on a relationship. I think it's a really special thing to find love. It's beautiful. Nothing can match it. But I want to make sure that I find other things in life that I love besides . . . love.

Vogue, **April 1, 2011**

MY FIRST KISS was in high school, and it was the worst thing ever. He pretty much dumped his entire saliva glands into my mouth. It traumatized me. I didn't kiss for, like, ever.

Rolling Stone, **April 14, 2011**

THE ONE THING [my grandmother] wants me to do is marry someone who loves me more than I love them. Because a woman will always give, and they'll always give even more than they need to. We're selfless beings. It's maternal. And even with a husband, she said it'll be that way with them as well, and they'll only meet you halfway if they love you a little more.

Oprah's Next Chapter, August 20, 2012

LOVE MAKES YOU go places you probably wouldn't ever go, had it not been for love. But I think everybody still has their limits.

GQ, November 13, 2012

I LIKE TO feel like a woman. I have to be in control in every other aspect of my life, so I feel like in a relationship, like I wanted to be able to take a step back and have somebody else take the lead.

GQ, November 13, 2012

NEVER UNDERESTIMATE A man's ability to make you feel guilty for his mistakes

Twitter post, December 13, 2012

I GET FEARFUL of relationships because I feel guilty about wanting someone to be completely faithful and loyal, when I can't even give them 10 percent of the attention that they need. It's just the reality of my time, my life, my schedule.

Vanity Fair, October 6, 2015

I MEAN I get horny, I'm human, I'm a woman, I want to have sex. But what am I going to do—just find the first random cute dude that I think is going to be a great ride for the night and then tomorrow I wake up feeling empty and hollow? . . . I can't do it to myself. I cannot. It has a little bit to do with fame and a lot to do with the woman that I am.

Vanity Fair, October 6, 2015

I'M TURNED ON by guys who are cultured. That'll keep me intrigued. They don't have to have a single degree, but they should speak other languages or know things about other parts of the world or history or certain artists or musicians.

T Magazine, October 12, 2015

THERE ARE PEOPLE in the world who will love you and people in the world who will hurt you, and there are people in the world who will do both.

GQ, December 15, 2009

THE PHYSICAL PAIN comes and it goes. The bruises fade away. But the thing that stays with you is the emotional scars.

GQ, December 15, 2009

WE JUST FELL really fast, and the more in love we became, the more dangerous we became for each other. Equally as dangerous, because it was a bit of an obsession.

on Chris Brown, *20/20*, November 6, 2009

WHEN I WAS in love, I fell so hard. I was really, really, really in love. The way it made me feel was priceless. And in a blink of an eye my whole life changed. Everything that I knew was different. I never thought I'd feel that pain in my life. I'm afraid of feeling that again.

on being assaulted by Chris Brown, *Harper's Bazaar*, July 6, 2012

I WAS HURT the most. Nobody felt what I felt. . . . It happened to me in front of the world. It was embarassing, it was humiliating, it was hurtful. It's not easy.

on being assaulted by Chris Brown, *Oprah's Next Chapter*, August 20, 2012

I DO THINK I'm a bit of a masochist. It's not something I'm proud of, and it's not something I noticed until recently. I think it's common for people who witness abuse in their household. They can never smell how beautiful a rose is unless they get pricked by a thorn.

Rolling Stone, April 14, 2011

I PUT UP my guard so hard. I didn't want people to see me cry. I didn't want people to feel bad for me. It was a very vulnerable time in my life, and I refused to let that be the image.

on being assaulted by Chris Brown, *Rolling Stone*, April 14, 2011

BEING LABELLED AS a victim was the hardest part for me. I didn't like feeling like a victim or weak, or having people feel sorry for me. . . . I just tried to put that away as much as I could.

on being assaulted by Chris Brown, *Skavlan*, September 8, 2014

I DON'T LIKE to talk about it. I never liked to talk about it, and that's why I never did—until recently because I felt like it was something that needed to be said to help young girls out there who are looking up to me.

> **on being assaulted by Chris Brown,**
> ***Jonathan Ross Show*, December 18, 2009**

I'LL SAY THAT to any young girl who's going through domestic violence: Don't react off of love. F love. Come out of the situation and look at it third-person and for what it really is, and then make your decision, because love is so blind.

> ***20/20*, November 6, 2009**

YOUNG GIRLS/WOMEN ALL over the world... we are a lot of things! We're strong innocent fun flirtatious vulnerable, and sometimes our innocence can cause us to be naïve! We always think it could NEVER be us, but in reality, it can happen to ANY of us! So ladies be careful and #listentoyomama! I love you and I care!

> **Twitter post, May 31, 2011**

IT TOOK A lot of strength to pull out of that relationship. To finally just officially cut it off. It was like night and day. It was two different worlds. It was the world I lived for two years, and then having the strength to say, "I'm gonna step into my own world. Start over."

on Chris Brown, *GQ*, December 15, 2009

PEOPLE CAN TELL. I'm in a much better place I think I've ever been in my life. Sometimes, you know, you have to go through really bad things to come out of it a better person. It has been a learning experience ever since that happened.

on being assaulted by Chris Brown, Hot 97 FM, November 24, 2009

THERE'S SO MANY reasons why I ever reconsidered having him in my life. He's not the monster everybody thinks. He's a good person. He has a fantastic heart. He's giving and loving. And he's fun to be around.

on reconciling with Chris Brown, *Rolling Stone*, February 14, 2013

OF COURSE EVERYBODY has their opinion about him, because of what he's done. That will always be there. But he made a mistake, and he's paid his dues. He's paid so much. And I know that's not a place he would ever want to go back to.

on reconciling with Chris Brown,
Rolling Stone, February 14, 2013

I THOUGHT I hated Chris, and I realized it was love that was tarnished. It looked like hate because it was ugly, it was angry, it was inflamed, it was tainted. And I realized that what it was is I had to forgive him because I cared about him still. And the minute I let go of that I started living again.

Oprah's Next Chapter, August 20, 2012

FOR ME, AND anyone who's been a victim of domestic abuse, nobody wants to even remember it. Nobody even wants to admit it. So to talk about it and say it once, much less 200 times, is like . . . I have to be punished for it? It didn't sit well with me.

Vanity Fair, October 6, 2015

I LOVE THE simple things but also the grand adventures. There's no pretentious my-brand-your-brand bullshit, it's just us living. I just feel like I can do any part of life by his side.

on her relationship with A$AP Rocky,
Vogue, May 1, 2022

WHAT I LOVE the most about us? Transparency with everything: how we're feeling, what our goals are, what our fears and insecurities are. The vulnerability to be able to say what you feel about each other.

on her relationship with A$AP Rocky,
Vogue, May 1, 2022

[Being a mom] is crazy. It is amazing. It is wild. It is weird. It is all of those things all at once. The best feeling. The most love I've ever known.

—*Savage X Fenty Show Vol. 4* red carpet, November 3, 2022

IT'S AMAZING TO have a friendship be the center of our entire family. I really love it.

on her relationship with A$AP Rocky, *Savage X Fenty*
Show Vol. 4 **red carpet, November 3, 2022**

I WOULD PREFER to have a full family. I'm pretty sure I could handle it if I had to on my own. But that's not what I'm striving for.

The Ellen Show, **November 14, 2012**

THE ONLY THING that matters is happiness, that's the only healthy relationship between a parent and a child. That's the only thing that can raise a child truly, is love.

British *Vogue*, **May 1, 2020**

I FEEL LIKE that's the type of mom I'm going to be. Psycho about it.

Elle, **March 15, 2022**

THEY'RE GOING TO teach me more than I could
ever teach them. And I want them to go for it. I
want to see who they are in the world, who they
become. Because I'm just here to keep them on
the rails—a passenger as much as a driver.

on her expected baby, *Vogue*, May 1, 2022

LIFE STARTS OVER when you become a parent.
It's like life that you've never known before. You
get a second full book. Not a chapter, it's like
a new book completely. The beginning is like
you're tripping acid every day. It's wild. Trippy as
hell.

***Savage X Fenty Show Vol. 4* red carpet,**
November 3, 2022

SEEING [MY SON'S] morning face—seeing a
baby with little bags, waking up, and they're just
like startled. They're trying to figure out where
they're at. It's the cutest. It's my favorite part of
the day.

***Savage X Fenty Show Vol. 4* red carpet,**
November 3, 2022

THE CHALLENGE IS we want to do regular shit with our baby. We want to go to the park. We want to go everywhere and take walks and things that we want to do as parents with him. But since we haven't gotten around to sharing him with the world, we have to navigate it extremely, extremely cautiously.

Savage X Fenty Show Vol. 4 **red carpet,**
November 3, 2022

THROW ME TO the wolves. Do what you want with me. But [my son] doesn't have a say in any of this. We've been protecting him thus far and you don't have any consent to be posting photos or selling photos of my child, a minor. Get the hell out of here with that.

on paparazzi taking photos of her son,
British *Vogue*, February 15, 2023

RAISING A YOUNG Black man is one of the scariest responsibilities in life. You're like, "What am I leaving my kids to? This is the planet they're gonna be living on?"

British *Vogue*, February 15, 2023

I'M LITERALLY THE girl trying to get into the boys club, waiting for my turn. [My son] is obsessed with his father. And I'm like: "Didn't I give birth to you? What is going on?"

British *Vogue*, February 15, 2023

WE'RE BEST FRIENDS with a baby. We have to be on the same page, but we've always kind of had that in our relationship. Everything changes when you have a baby but I wouldn't say it's done anything but made us closer.

on her relationship with A$AP Rocky,
British *Vogue*, February 15, 2023

Part II

RIHANNA

Music

SEEING ARTISTS LIKE B2K and JoJo come out at a young age really inspired me. If all of these young teenagers could do it, I thought I could, too.

The Honolulu Advertiser, September 15, 2006

[JAY-Z] DIDN'T WANT me to leave until I signed a deal. . . . Twelve hours later, I signed the deal. That was kind of crazy, right?

on auditioning for Def Jam Records,
The Honolulu Advertiser, September 15, 2006

A LOT OF people said I was going to be a one-hit wonder [with the song "Pon de Replay"]. But I worked my hardest to prove them wrong. And when we came out with the second album, "SOS" and "Unfaithful," both blew up!

The Honolulu Advertiser, September 15, 2006

MY FAVORITE SONG to sing in the shower was always "Vision of Love." Love Mariah Carey. Love her.

MTV News, January 1, 2007

WHITNEY HOUSTON, CELINE Dion, Mariah Carey, Shania Twain. I loved Luther Vandross. Still love him. And reggae was standard. You always listen to reggae in Barbados.

The Guardian, November 20, 2009

IN THE BEGINNING it was almost like I was just going along with a script that was written for me, and I didn't feel like an artist, I felt like a tool. I just felt, hey, here I am, this money-making vehicle for this big record label [and] I'm not even having fun, I'm not enjoying it, because I'm not able to be who I am. . . . Then, finally, I said, "You know what, if I want to do this, I'm going to do it my way" and I just rebelled, cut my hair, dyed it black, changed my image, changed my sound, and now we're still evolving.

The Guardian, November 20, 2009

I'm just a girl who loves to do music, loves to be creative. I love reggae music, I love hip-hop music, I love R&B. So I kind of fused everything together.

106 & Park, 2006

EVERY ALBUM FOR me has been a natural step in my growth. It has displayed the different steps in my career, and every one happens to be better than the previous one. And for me that's the most important thing—just making sure that every time you do something you do it better than before.

On the Record, **Fuse TV, November 26, 2009**

WITH THE GRAMMYS, it's really tricky because it's a small chance of winning. I just go into it not expecting to win because I hate to be disappointed.

Pre-Grammy Radio Session, January 30, 2010

I LOVE MAKING music. Music is what I do. I don't feel like there should be a break unless I choose to take a break.

BBC Radio 1, October 5, 2010

I JUST LOVED everything about what singing was, how it made me feel. I would sit my friends down and start running around with the hairbrush for a microphone. I would pretend I was making videos. The minute I discovered it, it became an obsession.

Vogue, April 1, 2011

GOOD GIRL GONE BAD was the first time I really took the reins in my career creatively. Then *Rated R* came right after that, and that's when I realized, OK, my fans love the music; now I need to get a little deep with them, get a little more vulnerable, open up.

Glamour, August 1, 2011

AND THE MUSIC we makin baby we makin for love

Twitter post, December 29, 2011

THAT'S WHY WOMEN are becoming so dominant in music right now, because we're very competitive beings, and we can not stand to see another woman do better than us. That bothers us a lot. As much as you guys have egos, our egos are a little bigger—we're just a lot better at hiding them.

Jonathan Ross Show, **March 6, 2012**

I'M ALWAYS LOOKING to make something new, something fresh, something that is different. I love travelling the world to find new producers that no one really knows of, and new sounds. That's why we switch it up every album because you have to.

BBC Radio 1, March 29, 2012

SINGING IS FAMILIAR. It's all I've ever known. Acting is a whole new world—and it's a world I respect as much, if not even more, because when you're a singer you get to be yourself, but when you act you really have to make people believe you're someone else.

BBC News, April 9, 2012

EVERY TIME I give [the fans] a little more, and now I feel like I am staring them right in their eyes because we pretty much made this album together. It's an incredible feeling.

"Rihanna – Road to *Talk That Talk* (Part 2),"
April 24, 2012

BECAUSE OF THE circumstances and how difficult it was to make this album and how much work we put into it, it feels that much better—a thousand times better to have the final product. And to not only share it with the world, but see people react the way they are. I could not customize that myself any better.

> **on the extremely busy schedule and heightened emotions she experienced in making *Talk That Talk*, "Rihanna – Road to *Talk That Talk* (Part 2)," April 24, 2012**

I ALWAYS WANT to make it interesting for them. I always want to make it a little fresh. A little ahead of what's on the radio and that's the challenge for me, but I enjoy that.

> **iHeartRadio, September 2012**

MADONNA IS ONE of those artists that was very self-expressive. She was bold, she was fearless— all those are things that I looked up to as a young woman. I wanted to be all those things. I wanted to really just be myself and feel free to express it and not be afraid of what people would think about it.

**Facebook Live with Bravo's Andy Cohen,
November 8, 2012**

MY FANS DEFINITELY have an impact on the way I make music [and] what I do.... They say things that you need to hear. They're out there in the world.... They know what's going on and you'd be stupid to be so oblivious to what they're saying.

**Facebook Live with Bravo's Andy Cohen,
November 8, 2012**

I sell out stadiums... Call it what ya want!!!

Instagram post, May 30, 2013

"NOBODY'S BUSINESS" [THE song] is basically the way I look at everything regarding my personal life. Even though you have to witness it—it's being documented at every second—it still is mine. . . . When it gets to my music and stuff like that, I'll give, and I'll give, and I'll give. And I just feel like I need to keep a little bit for me that I get to decide.

Facebook Live with Bravo's Andy Cohen,
November 8, 2012

I WANT TO make music that's hopeful, uplifting. Nothing corny or super sentimental. I just want it to have the feeling that brings you out of whatever you're going through. I want it to spark that fire. I want it to be real, authentic, and raw.

GQ, November 13, 2012

I DRAW INSPIRATION from everything. Even if it's weird, there's always something that you can find. The weirdest things are sometimes the coolest.

on making music, *The Ellen Show*, November 14, 2012

I HELD BACK before. I didn't show a lot of myself. I was very guarded. I needed to be open and free and fearless. Basically say, "Fuck it." What's the worst that can happen? They'll hate me? They've done that before.

on the album *Unapologetic*, *Complex*, January 14, 2013

IT WAS SO inspiring and uplifting. It was giving me hope, that song. I was tired of angry love songs. Love doesn't always have to be about breakups.

on the song "Diamonds," *Complex*, January 14, 2013

MAKING MUSIC IS like shopping for me. Every song is like a new pair of shoes. I love these I have, these look great—but what's new?

Rolling Stone, February 14, 2013

"STAY" I THINK is one of my favorite songs I've ever heard. I would think the same thing if it wasn't mine, cause I felt that way from a demo.

Rihanna 777 tour documentary, May 6, 2013

I NEVER EVEN knew genres of music. Only when I came here did people start putting a title on me, like, "Yeah you're pop; yeah you're pop-rock. You'd be great to be pop," or "You should stay urban." And it's like, huh? I didn't even know that that mattered. I thought everybody just played songs that were great.

Rihanna 777 tour documentary, May 6, 2013

I THINK A rockstar is more of an attitude, so even if you make pop music or pop fans love you, you're always seen as a rockstar because of who you are and how comfortable you are with being that.

Rihanna 777 tour documentary, May 6, 2013

IN THE CREATIVE world, inspiration is everything. There are three artists who have inspired me the most: Bob Marley, Tupac, and Aaliyah.

Styled to Rock (US Edition), October 25, 2013

I DID SING a lot as a child. A lot. I practiced hard to manuever my voice.

Vogue, February 17, 2014

I LOVE SINGING. I love it, and it doesn't feel like a chore. It's an expression. I never wanted to be famous. I just wanted my music to be heard all over the world.

Vogue, February 17, 2014

IT'S NOT ALL down to my voice. There's people with way more talent than I when it comes to singing. Bigger voices. But people want to know who you are. Fashion is a clear indication, a way to express your attitude, your mood.

Vogue, **February 17, 2014**

RECORDING A SONG . . . it feels like home.

Australian Today, **March 15, 2015**

I JUST WANTED to focus on things that felt real, that felt soulful, that felt forever. I wanted songs that I could perform in 15 years. I wanted an album that I could perform in 15 years, not any songs that were burnt out. I find that when I get on stage now I don't want to perform a lot of my songs because they don't feel like me. So I want to make songs that are timeless.

on the album *Anti*, *MTV News*, **March 16, 2015**

M<small>Y</small> <small>EIGHTH STUDIO</small> album [*Anti*] was a place for me to completely express myself creatively with no boundaries and try anything that I wanted.

T<small>HE THING THAT</small> made me fall in love with ["FourFiveSeconds"] is the juxtaposition of the music and the lyrics. When you read the lyrics it's a completely different song than what you are hearing. The music is easygoing, but the lyrical content is very loud and in your face. In performing this, the key was to make sure the aggression wasn't lost.

V Magazine, **April 21, 2015**

I<small>T'S EASY TO</small> make an album full of great songs. But I want people to go for the ride. The songs have to make sense together.

NME, **September 18, 2015**

I CAN'T MAKE a song for a particular person or demographic. If I love it, I'm gonna do it. I have to perform it for the rest of my life. A song is like a tattoo—you can never get away from it.

NME, September 18, 2015

TO ME IT'S never done until it's done. Until the final moment.

on finishing the album *Anti*, *NME*, September 18, 2015

THESE ARE PEOPLE who worked with the most talented people in the music industry, and I'm a little seed, from an island far away; to even have the opportunity to audition for them seemed so out of reach. I was terrified; my knees were shaking.

on auditioning for Def Jam Records, *Vanity Fair*, October 6, 2015

WHEN I STARTED making this album I never
would have imagined how much of a challenge
the process would be. I was evolving in the midst
of making a body of art that was supposed to
reflect who I was in that moment, yet it was
the very answer I didn't have! I was numb for a
while...numb to all the bullshit and numb to all
the good shit. But I was determined not to settle
for what everybody thought this should be, or
when they thought it should come, or how!

on the album *Anti*, Instagram post, January 28, 2017

WHEN I CAME to America, I found all these
different artists and genres. I finally knew what
Madonna actually looked like. I treated music
like it was candy. I could just pick up different
things and play with it.

British *Vogue*, September 1, 2018

AS AN ARTIST in this day and age, everything is driven by some kind of visual aspect. You want to push it and not have it be predictable.

British *Vogue*, September 1, 2018

IT'S REALLY ABOUT knowing that these people are there for you. They're there to see you because they love your music and you share that in common. Y'all are only meeting on that one premise. And that's it, you just go out there and that's exactly what you're going to give them.

**on performing in front of large crowds,
British *Vogue*, September 1, 2018**

MUSIC WAS MY gateway drug to every other wonderful aspect of creative opportunity that I've explored. And I'm grateful for that. But music is, and always will be, my first love and direct connection to your spirit.

Instagram post, January 29, 2019

Good Girl Gone Bad is where I started to take the reins: "I'm going to do whatever I want to do, I'm taking control of my vision, my sound, my clothes." I also embraced change along the way—things that make me a better woman, a better human being. Like, even the way I communicate: I'm really proud of my growth on that. I'm proud to walk into any building as this person. Nothing about me makes me embarrassed about me.

T Magazine, May 19, 2019

IT'S THE REASON why an album isn't being spat out like it used to. I used to be in the studio, only the studio, for three months straight, and an album would come out. Now, it's like a carousel. I do fashion one day, lingerie the next, beauty the next, then music the next.

Interview, June 10, 2019

MUSIC IS, LIKE, speaking in code to the world, where they get it. It's the weird langauge that connects me to them. Me the designer, me the woman who creates makeup and lingerie—it all started with music. It was my first pen pal-ship to the world. To cut that off is to cut my communication off. All of these other things flourish on top of that foundation.

Vogue, November 1, 2019

I FEEL LIKE I have no boundaries. I've done everything—I've done all the hits, I've tried every genre—now I'm just, I'm wide open. I can make anything that I want.

British *Vogue*, March 30, 2020

I AM *ALWAYS* working on music ... and when I'm ready to put it out in the way that I feel fit, it's gonna come out. You're not gonna be disappointed when it happens, it's gonna be worth it. I'm not gonna put it out just because people are waiting. It's taken this long, I'm gonna make it worth it.

Entertainment Tonight, July 29, 2020

YOU DO POP, you did this genre, you do that, you do radio, but now it's just like, what makes me happy? I just want to have fun with music. Everything is so heavy. The world that we live in is a lot. It's overwhelming every single day. And with the music, I'm using that as my outlet.

AP News, October 1, 2020

MUSIC IS ONE of those things where you can't rush it. You have to feel good about it. You have to love it. . . . It's personal, you know. It's more personal than an eye shadow. I picked a color and I picked a formula and I named it. But music is like my mind, my DNA, my soul. It's way more personal. So I want to take my time with that.

Savage X Fenty Show Vol. 3 **red carpet,**
September 22, 2021

IT KEEPS THE fire under my ass; I appreciate it. But I get it; I want it too.

on fans asking when her highly-anticipated ninth album
will come out, The Cut, September 23, 2021

In hindsight, [*Anti*] really is my most brilliant album. I say that because in the moment, I didn't realise it. But it always felt like the most cohesive album I've ever made.

British *Vogue*, February 15, 2023

IT'S AN ENTERTAINER'S dream to be on a stage like [the Super Bowl], but it's nerve-wracking. You want to get it right. You know everybody's watching, and they're rooting for you. . . . It's a challenge that I was willing to accept. Being a new mom, nothing would've gotten me out of the house if it wasn't a challenge like that.

Savage X Fenty Show Vol. 4 **red carpet,**
November 3, 2022

I'M DOING [THE Super Bowl] for the people that love my music, the people that have supported me and gotten me to this place in my career. And who miss me as a musician in particular.

British *Vogue*, **February 15, 2023**

I REALISED THAT if I keep waiting until this [ninth album] feels right and perfect and better, maybe it's going to keep taking forever and maybe it'll never come out and no, I'm not down to that. So I want to play. And by play, I mean I have my ideas in my head, but I can't say them out loud yet.

British *Vogue*, **February 15, 2023**

Fame

REMEMBERED AS RIHANNA! Remembered as being the artist from the Carribean who came here and made it. I made it internationally. Just remember it's me.

when asked what she wants to be remembered for at the end of her career, *MTV News*, October 2005

BEFORE, YOUNG GIRLS would look at me, and they thought my life was perfect, but now they realise that it's not. Nobody's perfect. I'm living the same human life that they are, just with a more public career—and when they realise that I do go through dumb stuff like that—all of a sudden that makes me human for them. So now I feel really strong, but I also feel very open.

on being assaulted by Chris Brown, *The Guardian*, November 20, 2009

I BUILT A brand. The brand is Rihanna. And there are a lot things that come with that. It's a lot of work that went into this brand, and that's why I say I built an empire, because it was from the ground up, you know. We started from scratch.

On the Record, Fuse TV, November 26, 2009

YOU CAN'T STEP out of your hotel room without the paparazzi being parked out there. They're parked outside of your house. There's no moment of "Okay, now I'm finished where I can close the door." . . . That's the big downside. But also, if that's what I have to deal with to do what I love, I'll take it.

On the Record, Fuse TV, November 26, 2009

IN THE BEGINNING of my career, I remember "Pon de Replay" started doing really well and he [Jay-Z] came up to me at a showcase and he said, "You must be a really great person because great things keep happening for you. Don't ever change who you are. Always remain humble, the same." And it kind of rings in my ear. Every day I hear that.

On the Record, **Fuse TV, November 26, 2009**

I JUST THINK people straight up don't know who I am; they just know what I look like, they know the idea of me. But—they'll learn more this time, because now I let my guard down, and I'm more comfortable just being myself. That's exactly what I want to be.

GQ, **December 15, 2009**

THE MOST FUN things that I do are the most normal, simple things, things that most people take for granted—like being able to watch TV and lounge around the house, or having a really good meal. I love going to the grocery store—for me, that's like an event!

Seventeen, August 1, 2010

I'VE STRUGGLED WITH it and have come to the conclusion that I can only live my life for me. I definitely want to help and teach little girls whenever I can, but then there is the character that I have to play in my videos to tell stories. It's art. And a lot of the parts that I play aren't necessarily what I stand for in real life. But it's hard to differentiate that sometimes.

on the expectation to be a role model,
Vogue, April 1, 2011

THE MINUTE I discovered that freedom and started toying with it, I loved it so much that it felt real for the first time. When something feels real, you don't make any apologies for it. When it feels good to you, nothing else matters. Everything else is just noise.

on discovering the freedom to express herself, *Vogue*,
April 1, 2011

I HATE THAT my business is out there, but at the same time, if the media had never found out about certain situations, I would still be in them.

Rolling Stone, April 14, 2011

WHEN I THINK about it, I really do take some pleasure in the negativity. I don't want to say turned on by it—but I'm turned on by it.

Rolling Stone, April 14, 2011

[JAY-Z] THREW ME out there but he guided every step of the way. He told me that the only way people can get to me is through my circle. If my circle is phony, then stuff will get to me.

Complex, May 11, 2011

THE MUSIC INDUSTRY isn't exactly Parents R Us! We have the freedom to make art, LET US! It's your job to make sure [your kids] don't turn out like US

**on backlash for the violent "Man Down" music video,
Twitter post, June 2, 2011**

I FEEL LIKE pop stars can't be rock stars anymore because they have to be role models, and it takes the fun out of it for us, because we just want to have fun with art.

Glamour, August 1, 2011

PEOPLE—ESPECIALLY WHITE PEOPLE—THEY want me to be a role model just because of the life I lead. The things I say in my songs, they expect it of me and [being a role model] became more of my job than I wanted it to be. But no, I just want to make music. That's it.

British *Vogue*, November 1, 2011

I DON'T EVER want to be a theme, because then it belongs to someone, and that's not right. I want to cultivate something that's part of my personal swagger—whatever my mojo tells me, that's what I'm going to do.

British *Vogue*, November 1, 2011

SOCIETY USED TO be about doing things, thoughts and ideas...now it's about being someone

Twitter post, December 28, 2011

I'D LOVE TO go somewhere where nobody
really cares.

on whether she's been anywhere where no one
recognized her, BBC Radio 1, March 29, 2012

I'M SUPER DUPER afraid of the pedestal that
comes with fame and being a celebrity. So I keep
myself as close to the ground as possible.

Oprah's Next Chapter, August 20, 2012

I WANT TO be a peer to my fans. I don't ever want
to be above them or think that because they're
fans I'm not one of them or they're not one of us.
We're all people.

Oprah's Next Chapter, August 20, 2012

I don't like to live a calculated life. I don't do anything for the reaction.

Vogue, October 14, 2012

I'M VERY FREE when it comes to Twitter. I like being able to just say it. I don't want to paint the picture for people. I want them to read between the lines. But I'll give them what's on my mind, and by putting the pieces together they'll slowly start to figure me out a little better.

Oprah's Next Chapter, August 20, 2012

IT CAN BE very easy to be led astray or caught up and sucked into the fame, and bright lights, and everything being great. It can be easy to do that. But I have great people around me—a lot of people I've known since my childhood and a lot of people I trust.

Facebook Live with Bravo's Andy Cohen,
November 8, 2012

SOMETIMES A PERSON looks at me and sees dollars. They see numbers and they see a product. I look at me and see art.

GQ, November 13, 2012

PEOPLE TAKE THE little bit of information they're fed, and they draw a picture of who you are. Most of the time it's wrong.

Complex, January 14, 2013

I CAN'T MAKE everybody happy, but at the end of the day, if my fans are happy, that's all I fucking care about.

Rihanna 777 tour documentary, May 6, 2013

IT'S NOT EASY what we do; it's very difficult at times. It's a lot of pressure to be a lot of things, and I've never felt comfortable being anything but myself.

Best Fan Army Award acceptance speech at iHeartRadio Music Awards, May 1, 2014

YOU TAKE ON the persona of an adult because you have to make a lot of adult decisions. It's a career that I have a lot of control, a lot of say in. It's not a children's industry, so you have to act like an adult and think like an adult, and at times feel like one.

Skavlan, September 8, 2014

EVERY DAY IT'S something else. After a while you kind of become numb. At first, everything bothers you. . . . But after a while you just give up. You can't keep chasing it. They'll keep saying it, so you just have to live your life as though they don't exist.

on negative media, *Skavlan*, September 8, 2014

EVERY TIME THERE'S paparazzi pulling up outside the building there's anxiety. I can't say I'm numb to it, because it never feels normal. But it's not surprising, either.

NME, September 18, 2015

I HONESTLY THINK how much fun it would be to live my reputation. People have this image of how wild and crazy I am, and I'm not everything they think of me. The reality is that the fame, the rumors—this picture means this, another picture means that—it really freaks me out.

Vanity Fair, October 6, 2015

THERE'S A LONG way to fall when you pretend that you're so far away from the earth, far away from reality, floating in a bubble that's protected by fame or success. It's scary, and it's the thing I fear the most: to be swallowed up by that bubble. It can be poison to you, fame.

Vanity Fair, October 6, 2015

I USED TO feel unsafe right in the moment of an accomplishment—I felt the ground fall from under my feet because this could be the end. And even now, while everyone is celebrating, I'm on to the next thing. I don't want to get lost in this big cushion of success.

T Magazine, October 12, 2015

MY FANS, I love you so much. You have no idea. You keep me driven. You keep this thing special.

Icon Award acceptance speech at American Music Awards, November 24, 2013

IT IS A very surreal feeling. It's almost like I can't touch it.... It still doesn't feel real because I feel like I have so much more to do.

on winning the Icon Award, *Good Morning America*, January 9, 2016

MY SUCCESS, IT started as my dream, but now
my success is not my own—it's my family's,
it's my fans', it's the Caribbean as a whole, it's
women, it's Black women.

**Michael Jackson Vanguard Award acceptance speech at
MTV Video Music Awards, August 28, 2016**

PEOPLE DON'T KNOW that I'm shy.

Interview, June 10, 2019

I STARTED OFF as a kid, so I know my fans were
kids, too. We're all growing up together. It's crazy
to see where our paths are taking us.

Interview, June 10, 2019

WHEN YOU KEEP yourself up at night thinking
about how to make history, you're not gonna
make it.

Savage X Fenty Show Vol. 1, **September 20, 2019**

Personal

Philosophy

I ALWAYS FELT like I was a leader. I had to do what I felt was perfect for me. I didn't do it because it looked cool to somebody else.

MTV News, **January 1, 2007**

I'M A MUSICIAN. I'm a very creative person. I love music. I love fashion. I'm very edgy. I'm always a little to the left, never safe, because it's just not me, it's never who I am. And everything I do, it reflects that, whether it be what I wear in an interview, a photo shoot, nothing is safe cause that's just not Rihanna.

On the Record, **Fuse TV, November 26, 2009**

"NEVER A FAILURE, always a lesson." It's something that's always been said around me— something that my best friend Melissa and I really keep strong. It's our mantra to life.

on her tattoo, *Seventeen,* **August 1, 2010**

I HATE DRAMA. But at the same time, nothing bothers me more than when life's perfect. And that's the sick part. I just love a challenge.

Glamour, **August 1, 2011**

YOU KNOW, I'VE tried so many things, I've gone through the stage of having other people decide for me. Now I don't have anyone else decide for me. I have a lot of clarity in my life now, more than ever before. And it's nice being myself.

British *Vogue*, November 1, 2011

SURE U WISH u did some things differently, but no sense in becoming burdened with regret over things u have no power to change

Twitter post, February 25, 2012

I'M VERY COMPETITIVE with myself. And I don't like staying in the same place. I like growth. And personal growth is important to me. And I take that through my career.

DayBreak, **March 29, 2012**

DOING WHAT YOU want means moving forward with the way you feel and living your truth. And a lot of the time you'll find common ground with people, and sometimes there are a lot of people you won't find that agree with you. But it has to be your truth because that's the only way, really.

Extra, **April 30, 2012**

PEOPLE HESITATE TO follow their desires because they don't know how to divide their soul from their spirit

Twitter post, June 15, 2012

LIFE WITHOUT PURPOSE is vanity.

Twitter post, August 6, 2012

I HAD TO fake it until I made it. That's what I had
to do. I had to pretend I was comfortable when I
was not.

Oprah's Next Chapter, **August 20, 2012**

TIME HEALS ALL, and heels hurt to wait in

Instagram post, July 12, 2012

THOUGHT FOR THE day: The thing that we most
avoid doing, is very often the thing we should
do most!

Twitter post, July 31, 2012

YOU NEVER KNOW which minute is the last one,
just 60 seconds!

Twitter post, August 31, 2012

I DON'T GET bitter, I just get better

Twitter post, September 26, 2012

SOMETIMES YA GOTTA do whatcha gotta do to get it done

Instagram post, November 24, 2012

I DON'T GO out of my way to be a rebel or to have that perception, but a lot of the decisions I make, a lot of the direction I want to move, is against the grain, or against society's tight lane, and I'm aware of that sometimes. It might not be fitting with the norm, but that's OK for me.

Vogue, **February 17, 2014**

I HAVE A very firm relationship with God and I believe in Jesus, and I stick to that.

Vogue, **February 17, 2014**

I can only
do me. And
nobody else
is going to
be able to
do that.

Vogue, April 1, 2016

DIFFERENT THINGS IN life happen, and they change the course of your plan, they change your life, they change everything about your life. And the only thing you can do is hold on to who you are.

Skavlan, **September 8, 2014**

FUCK BITCHES, GET money!

on her mantra, *Elle*, **November 3, 2014**

EVERY DAY WE wake up, means we get another chance at life....to live what we've learned and to discover even more, to be good to other people and to know that you are a part of their smile!

Instagram post, February 20, 2015

I RUN AWAY from anything that does not stimulate me. I often find myself gravitating toward the underground. There is a certain creative freedom there that you can't experience anywhere else.

V Magazine, April 21, 2015

I TAKE RISKS because I get bored. And I get bored very easily.

NME, September 18, 2015

I JUST HAVE a way of breaking the rules even when I don't intend to.

NME, September 18, 2015

WHEN I SEE myself as an old woman, I just think about being happy. And hopefully, I'll still be fly.

NME, September 18, 2015

MY THOUGHTS NEVER bore me. I like to spend my time alone wisely. A moment of quiet. A moment of silence. A moment of just organising my thoughts. I just enjoy being alone.

NME, September 18, 2015

I LOVE HAVING fun, but you have to be responsible, you have to be safe, protect yourself. You have to look out for yourself because nobody else can do that for you.

Good Morning America, January 9, 2016

I BELIEVE GOD put us all here for a reason, and we all have our purpose, and we are here to fulill our purpose individually. I think the thing that's kept me sane, the thing that's kept me humble, the thing that's kept me successful is being myself.

BGR Rock Star Award acceptance speech at BLACK GIRLS ROCK!, April 6, 2016

You mean KFC on a private jet is not normal?

Elle, **September 26, 2017**

You've just got to laugh at yourself, honestly.

Vogue, **May 3, 2018**

I think confidence is something you kind of grow into. And as you get older, you don't think about things the same way.

Australian Today, **October 5, 2018**

It starts with self-love. I think people get so caught up in the outside influences, especially with social media today, they're always looking for validation from the world. And I feel like when you're happy and you love yourself, no one can take that from you, and it doesn't even matter who likes it.

on empowering yourself as a woman, *Studio 10*,
October 3, 2018

I've never been afraid to take risks. That's the thing that got me out of my own way.

Vogue, October 9, 2019

WHEN YOU HEAR the word "savage" it's pretty self-explanatory. You know, it's a confident word. It's a word that is fearless. . . . And I feel like every woman has a savage inside of 'em. Whether they've found it or not, it's there.

behind the scenes of the Savage X Fenty show at
New York Fashion Week, September 13, 2018

STRENGTH, LOVE, FORGIVENESS, sacrifice, hard work & helping others in any way you can is what true beauty looks like.

Twitter post, April 5, 2019

THE DEVIL JUST has a way of making you feel like you're not good enough, and that you're not worthy of god being close to you. It's really not the truth, but you wind up feeling like that.

Interview, June 10, 2019

IT'S ONLY THE last couple years that I started to realize that you need to make time for yourself, because your mental health depends on it. If you're not happy, you're not going to be happy even doing things that you love doing. It'd feel like a chore. I never want work to feel like a chore. My career is my purpose, and it should never feel like anything other than a happy place.

Interview, June 10, 2019

ART IS ALL that you are, it's all that you think. It's all that you're made of.

Savage X Fenty Show Vol. 1, September 20, 2019

THIS YEAR HAS been quite an overwhelming one, and I'm working on that ish called Balance.

Instagram post, November 13, 2019

I GUESS THERE'S a lot of discomfort based on the barriers that the society puts on you, what they tell you you should be, shouldn't be, look like, not look like, talk like, dress like. And to just be okay with whatever it is that you feel and are, that to me is the ultimate freedom.

E! News, February 8, 2020

INSPIRATIONALLY IT'S ME, what I'm pulling in. It's like, what do I want to bring into my spirit, my mind, my logic, my being, my ideas, my creative space? That's where the inspiration goes. I want that to come in and, in a way, it comes in one way and it's evoked through my art in another way and that could be inspiration for someone else in the future.

Vogue, August 26, 2020

[SEXUALITY IS] YOUR own divine inner power, whether it's finding it, whether it's sharing it, or just being it.

Savage X Fenty Show Vol. 2, October 2, 2020

HAPPINESS KIND OF is the open door to everything. Like you could do anything. You could be creative, you could be savage, you could be anti-social, you could just be whatever you want as long as you're comfortable, you're happy being exactly in that space.

The Hollywood Fix, April 16, 2021

I'VE GROWN TO appreciate the little things. And I've grown to love being still.

The Hollywood Fix, April 16, 2021

YOU BE FEARLESS every day and when you don't feel like it, just pretend, girl.

Savage X Fenty Show Vol. 3 red carpet,
September 22, 2021

I think confidence is key. Confidence can make anyone sexy.

Savage X Fenty Show Vol. 3 red carpet, September 22, 2021

I'm still pinching myself for where I'm at every day.

Savage X Fenty Show Vol. 3 red carpet, September 22, 2021

What's another word for Savage? RIHLENTLESS!!

Twitter post, October 3, 2021

Part III

FENTY

Beauty and

Business

YOU HAVE TO just accept your body. You may not love it all the way, but you just have to be comfortable with it. Comfortable with knowing that that's your body, you know. You just want something else that someone else has. But that doesn't mean what you have isn't beautiful.

DayBreak, March 29, 2012

MEANWHILE ON SET being able to do hair and being able to do black hair are 2 different things! #magazines please pay attention!

Twitter post, September 26, 2012

BLACK IZ BEAUTIFUL.

Instagram post, August 3, 2015

I LOVE BLACK hair on me. I love it and I love to cut it short and be edgy and have fun with it.

Alan Carr: Chatty Man, April 3, 2017

WHEN I HAVE a tan, and when my skin is really good—no breakouts—and usually in humid weather. I guess that's really me describing Barbados.

> on when she feels most beautiful, **New York Fashion Week**, *E!* **Red Carpet, September 8, 2017**

FOUNDATION WAS THE first product I ever owned. It was like magic, and I've been in love with makeup ever since.

> *Elle*, **September 26, 2017**

LIPSTICK ALWAYS GOT me in trouble. Whether it was at home as a kid, or my early teenage years in my career, I always had the urge to wear it. So I broke all those rules. Now lipstick is like my li'l secret weapon!

> *Elle*, **September 26, 2017**

I LIKE MY makeup to look like skin—really
good skin.

InStyle, November 6, 2017

MAKEUP IS THERAPEUTIC for me. Once I start
my glam—the makeup, the hair—I'm good. I'll
play music, find the good light in the bathroom,
and just have a great time. That's what gets
me motivated.

InStyle, November 6, 2017

I HAVE 100 percent involvement in this process
[of creating the Fenty Beauty products], which
is what makes this so special and very fun. I
have so much creative freedom from products
to packaging, and that's really the only way this
brand will stay true to my vision for it.

TIME, November 16, 2017

MY DAY-TO-DAY REALLY depends on my mood. It depends on the occasion, it depends on how lazy I'm feeling that day, how much in a rush I am. You know, who I'm going to see. It all determines what kind of makeup I do, if I do makeup, and how much makeup I'm going to wear.

Vogue, "Rihanna's Epic 10-Minute Guide to Going-Out Makeup," May 3, 2018

I THINK THE best teacher is yourself. You have to practice on your own face. Because there are going to be things that you can do better than makeup artists. There's a certain point where they hand you something [and] you do it, because there's one way that you like it and one way that it works.

Vogue, "Rihanna's Epic 10-Minute Guide to Going-Out Makeup," May 3, 2018

I DIDN'T REALLY expect people to have this emotional connection to the [Fenty Beauty] brand because they've discovered their skin in a bottle, on a shelf, for the first time. It's the thing that brings me closer, even now, to the customer.

British *Vogue*, September 1, 2018

I'LL NEVER FORGET the day [my mom] let me wear makeup for the first time. It was for a school pageant, and it was a wrap after that. I never fell out of love with makeup since that day.

***Australian Today*, October 2, 2018**

I LOVE TO create, and I'm only going to create things that I love, not things that I think I should do because I'm at a place in my career. I love makeup. Makeup has been a huge part of my career from day one. And so to be able to create that and make it the way you want it, knowing all the things you've seen and all the mistakes you've seen with other brands, I wanted to make something of my own.

Studio 10, October 3, 2018

WE ARE ALWAYS on the lookout for the ones who still haven't found their shade, because nothing is more important to us than making sure no shade is left behind

Instagram post, January 11, 2019

I DIDN'T EVEN really know how bad it was, the void in the market for dark foundation, because all I'd seen was black women put makeup on. I don't even think 40 shades is enough! And so I added 10 more recently, and we're not gonna stop there.

T Magazine, May 19, 2019

[E]VERY COLLABORATION I did outside of music, I used Fenty so that you didn't have to hear the word "Rihanna" every time you say something that I did. So Rihanna stayed the music, the person. But these other brands are called Fenty.

T Magazine, May 19, 2019

I'M SHOCKED BY people saying, "Oh my god, what made you think of making makeup for black girls?" I'm like, "What? You thought this was like, a marketing strategy? Like I'm a genius?" It's shocking most of the time. Then it turns into disappointment that this is groundbreaking right now. In my mind, this was just normal.

British *Vogue*, May 1, 2020

I NEVER THOUGHT I'd make this much money, so a number is not going to stop me from working. I'm not being driven by money right now. Money is happening along the way, but I'm working out of what I love to do, what I'm passionate about.

T Magazine, May 19, 2019

THE THING THAT keeps me alive and passionate is being creative. With every business outlet, I'm making something from a vision to a reality, and that's the thing I really enjoy.

Interview, June 10, 2019

THERE WILL BE no stone left unturned. I am serious about my makeup. I want you to come into Sephora, stop at the Fenty Beauty counter, and leave.

on expanding the Fenty Beauty product range,
"Artistry and Beauty Talk with Rihanna,"
Fenty Beauty, July 8, 2019

WHOEVER TOLD YOU skincare has a gender, LIED to you!

Twitter post, July 14, 2020

THAT'S RIGHT BABY…@FENTYSKIN is for my fellas too! No matter who you are, you deserve to have great skin! 🔥

Twitter post, July 19, 2020

MAKING @FENTYSKIN WAS a challenge to cover all bases and thinking of the many skin types that are out there! But y'all know I love a good challenge

Twitter post, July 27, 2020

AS AN ISLAND girl, fortunately, I had lots of access to key ingredients that work really well for your skin. … I tried to keep that a huge part of the process with ingredients.

on Fenty Skin, Marie Claire, August 1, 2020

I'VE ALWAYS SEEN the Fenty brand as more than just makeup, and I knew I wanted to make skin care from the very beginning. It was just about getting it right. You have to live with the formulas for awhile and test them in different ways. It's very different from makeup in that sense. It takes a long time.

Harper's Bazaar, **August 4, 2020**

FOR ME, THE product I would splurge on the most is moisturizer, anything to do with moisture, whether it's face or body. I think adding good moisture to your skin and having something that you know is effective and works— super important for everyone, every skin type, every skin tone.

Harper's Bazaar, **August 4, 2020**

Rule number one: Wash your face every damn day.

"Rihanna's Morning Skincare Routine,"
Fenty Skin, August 13, 2020

MY ENTIRE CONCEPT of beauty came from [my mom]. I was always so intrigued by her. I wanted to dress like her. I wanted to look like her. I wanted to do my hair like her, do my makeup like her. She was a sales clerk for beauty products and perfume and makeup. It's so weird that it's come full circle that all of these ventures are things that I've extended my creativity to and that has been a part of my brand overall.

Vogue, "Rihanna Answers 15 Questions From
A$AP Rocky," August 26, 2020

THE TOPIC OF inclusivity has become something that our brand has fallen upon just by sincere and organic perspective. My idea of beauty has always been like a Black woman. So the way that I've expanded that idea was doing skincare in a more gender-neutral idea where men feel included as well.

Vogue, "Rihanna Answers 15 Questions From
A$AP Rocky," August 26, 2020

IT REALLY IS inspiring to me how you can use colors, paint, makeup, textures just to embody whatever you want to. I watch drag queens do the same thing when they draw on their lips, and all of a sudden their entire demeanor changes. You can see the confidence, you can feel the confidence. There's a huge emotional attachment to that, and there's an empowerment within that.

Savage X Fenty Show Vol. 2, October 2, 2020

BROWN IS MY favorite color. Brown is who I am. Brown is what I come from. If I'm going to make a fragrance that represents me, even the body language of the bottle needs to marry that. So, I wanted something brown, but also transparent— so you could see the liquid and the fragrance you're about to experience.

Fenty Eau de Parfum press release, August 2, 2021

You know, it was real weird getting congralutations texts from people for money. I was just like, wait, I've never gotten congratulated for money before. That shit is crazy. But it made sense when I realized that it was inspiring to people, that they felt like this is something that they could achieve, knowing where I've come from, knowing my humble beginnings.

**on hitting billionaire status, *Savage X Fenty Show Vol. 3*
red carpet, September 22, 2021**

If you have on a good strong lipstick, it changes everything.

**"Fenty Icon Semi-Matte Refillable Lipstick"
Fenty Beauty, February 7, 2022**

Fenty Beauty, our brand, is for everyone. We want everyone to feel included.

***Elle*, March 15, 2022**

THERE'S A PREGNANCY glow. There's also those days, girl. Especially in the third trimester where you wake up and you're like, oh, do I have to get dressed? Makeup for sure helps you feel like a real person.

Elle, March 15, 2022

FRAGRANCE IN SKINCARE for me is so important because it's a crucial part of the experience. It's a huge part of it. It's a huge part of the texture, the lathering, whether you're patting on toner—I want you to always feel triggered and have an emotion connected to that experience.

"Behind Fenty Skin With Rihanna," Fenty Skin, July 1, 2022

I WAS BACK at work three days after I gave birth.

Savage X Fenty Show Vol. 4 red carpet, November 3, 2022

Fashion and Style

I GOT DESPERATE for things that weren't available in Barbados. I would cut things out of magazines. I was obsessed with creating a visual with clothing, and the way things are combined.

Vogue, **April 1, 2011**

IT'S BECOME MORE about taking a risk. When I am putting looks together, I dare myself to make something work. I always look for the most interesting silhouette or something that's a little off, but I have to figure it out. I have to make it *me*. I think that's the thrill in fashion.

Vogue, **April 1, 2011**

IT'S FLATTERING. YES, it's inaccurate but flattering.

on being named "Sexiest Woman Alive" by *Esquire*,
Oprah's Next Chapter, **August 19, 2012**

MUSIC DOESN'T GO without fashion.

Styled to Rock **(UK Edition), October 16, 2012**

WHEN I WAS thirteen or fourteen, I didn't want to wear what my mom wanted me to wear. I was very much a boy in my style, my demeanor. All my friends were guys. I loved things that boys did. I loved being easy with my clothes. I loved wearing hats and scarves and snapbacks on my head. It was my way of rebelling.

Vogue, **March 1, 2014**

YOU WILL NEVER be stylish if you don't take risks.

Vogue, **March 1, 2014**

WHEN IT FEELS like it's yours and it feels like it's you, that's what works. You want to look like you are not just someone in cool clothes.

Vogue, **March 1, 2014**

I GREW UP in a really small island, and I didn't have a lot of access to fashion. But as far as I can remember, fashion has always been my defense mechanism.

Style Icon Award acceptance speech at CFDA
Fashion Awards, June 2, 2014

EVEN AS A child, I remember thinking: "She can beat me, but she cannot beat my outfit." And to this day, that is how I think about it. I can compensate for all my weaknesses with my fashion.

Style Icon Award acceptance speech at CFDA
Fashion Awards, June 2, 2014

I WANTED TO wear something that looked like it was floating on me. But after that, I thought, O.K., we can't do this again for a while. No nipples, no sexy shit, or it's going to be like a gimmick. That night [at the CFDA awards] was like a last hurrah; I decided to take a little break from that and wear clothes.

> **on the infamous sheer gown covered in Swarovski crystals worn to the CFDA awards, *Vanity Fair*, October 6, 2015**

COULD YOU IMAGINE the CFDA dress with a bra? I would slice my throat. I already wanted to, for wearing a thong that wasn't bedazzled. That's the only regret I have in my life.

> **on the infamous sheer gown covered in Swarovski crystals worn to the CFDA awards, *Vogue*, April 1, 2016**

ALL OF MY favorite artists and fashion icons and models are from the nineties. Everybody was just so fearless.

> ***Vogue*, April 1, 2016**

I WAS ALREADY proud to be a Dior woman, but to be a black Dior woman and the first: It did something else for me.

Vogue, **April 1, 2016**

POT NEVER GOES out of style.

on wearing a cannabis-print onesie, *Alan Carr: Chatty Man*, April 3, 2017

I GET BORED really easily, so I love when things can trigger an inspiration in my mind. Things I love the most are the things that I get jealous that I didn't think of or come up with myself. Young, fresh, new perspective.

on wearing new designers, *W Magazine*, October 13, 2017

SAVAGES COME IN all shapes and sizes!!

on Savage X Fenty, Instagram post, April 29, 2018

SAVAGE IS REALLY about taking complete ownership of how you feel and the choices you make. Basically making sure everybody knows the ball is in your court.

Vogue, **June 1, 2018**

AS WOMEN, WE'RE looked at as the needy ones, the naggy ones, the ones who are going to be heartbroken in a relationship. Savage is just the reverse.

Vogue, **June 1, 2018**

I'M NOT BUILT like a Victoria's Secret girl, and I still feel very beautiful and confident in my lingerie.

Vogue, **June 1, 2018**

TO ALL MY savages, I love you and I love the movement we have made together!

Twitter post, May 1, 2019

I USE MYSELF as the muse. It's sweatpants with pearls, or a masculine denim jacket with a corset. I feel like we live in a world where people are embracing every bit of who they are. Look at Jaden Smith, Childish Gambino. They dare you to tell them not to.

T Magazine, May 19, 2019

I LIKE TO think of my establishment at the Fenty house as a hub. So I am always looking at grad collections, who's about to leave college, who wants a year here. And we've done that with a couple young designers and a couple new ones that are coming in. Even if you've never designed something in your life, you might have impeccable taste: I'm welcoming everyone's vision here, because that's what it's gonna take. I can't just think I know everything.

on Fenty fashion house under LVMH, *T Magazine*, May 19, 2019

My ultimate style advice? Play. . . . That's what fashion is about, it's not that serious. It's drag.

Vogue France, May 24, 2019

THREE WORDS FOR my style: Moody, for one. I get bored really easily—I don't know what you would call that in one word. Also, daring.

Vogue France, **May 24, 2019**

IT'S REALLY SOMETIMES not about your closet. You could have all the clothes in the world and it's like, what does my body want to wear today?

Vogue, **May 30, 2019**

I'M A CONTROL freak so I do everything. I see everything. There's not one step of the way, there's not one lace trim, there's not one bra strap, there's not one hardware color, there is not one bow on a panty that I do not see and approve, not one copy online that I don't see and approve.

Savage X Fenty show at New York Fashion Week red carpet, September 10, 2019

I WANT WOMEN to feel confident no matter what size they are, no matter what shade of nude they are, no matter what their personality is, what their race is, their religion is. I want women to feel confident and sexy because that's who we are and we deserve to feel like that.

Savage X Fenty show at New York Fashion Week
red carpet, September 10, 2019

YOU BELONG IN these pieces. You, me, trans women, women of all sizes, paraplegic women, *all women are important women!* All women belong here.

Elle, **September 11, 2019**

I WILL DANCE in these [Savage X Fenty] pieces in my kitchen until we get it right!

Elle, **September 11, 2019**

THERE'S NO RULES with designing lingerie. You can do anything, you can go as far as you want, you can go as comfortable as you want. You can go as sexy as you want. And it's just a whole new outlet of creating, making things from scratch.

Savage X Fenty Show Vol. 1, **September 20, 2019**

YOU CAN BE both introverted and extroverted in fashion because in any creative outlet, you can hide behind the art and yet you're screaming through it.

Savage X Fenty Show Vol. 1, **September 20, 2019**

I'M NOT THE face of my brand, but I am the muse, and my DNA has to run all the way through it. I don't want anyone to pull up my website and think, Rihanna would never wear that.

on **Savage X Fenty**, *Vogue*, **November 1, 2019**

I ENJOY [A non-binary style]. That's what Fenty [fashion house] really stands for. We have a lot of unisex styles. And I shop mostly in the men's section, so when making my clothes that was always in mind: like, I want guys to love my stuff too.

Entertainment Tonight, **February 7, 2020**

[FASHION IS] ALWAYS something that I've been interested in and to have this opportunity to do a Fenty brand with LVMH is special. It's special. It makes me feel validated.

on Fenty fashion house under LVMH,
***Entertainment Tonight,* February 7, 2020**

THE JOURNEY'S BEEN incredible. It's a lot of hard work and just being true to your brand and I've always tried to stay and stick with things that I enjoy doing.

on Fenty fashion house under LVMH,
***Entertainment Tonight,* February 7, 2020**

WHETHER IT'S CLOTHING, lingerie, or skincare, my goal is always to include all women.

Marie Claire, August 1, 2020

WHEN I IMAGINE something, I imagine everyone that I know and love being a part of it. I want to make stuff that I can see on the people that I know, and they come in all different shapes, sizes, races, religions.

Savage X Fenty Show Vol. 2, October 2, 2020

INSPIRATION CAN COME from anything. What makes it unique is your own interpretation on that message, that color scheme, that texture, and so everything that I do is gonna be personal to me, when it comes to Savage, especially.

Savage X Fenty Show Vol. 2, October 2, 2020

WHETHER IT'S JAPAN or Paris or the U.S., wherever I see a fabric, the first thing I want to do is touch it. And I get into a lot of trouble at museums because of that.

Savage X Fenty Show Vol. 2, **October 2, 2020**

DISPLAYING SEXUALITY HAS become something that's way deeper than surface for me. . . . Sexuality is personal. It is something that has to be owned or earned. Sometimes it's tainted because you've had horrible experiences or been robbed of your own power.

Savage X Fenty Show Vol. 2, **October 2, 2020**

PEOPLE REALLY ENJOYED just seeing a bit of inclusivity. And when we realized how much people appreciated something that we just sincerely wanted to do, we didn't know that we would have the response that we did, and so we took that and we said, this is going to be the core of what our brand stands for.

on Savage X Fenty, *The Hollywood Fix*, April 16, 2021

I'M ALWAYS LIKE, what's next, what's next.
I want something better. I want something
different. It doesn't necessarily have to be bigger,
but maybe it's deeper. Maybe we just go deeper
and explore things that aren't being discussed.

on Savage X Fenty, *The Hollywood Fix*, April 16, 2021

BEHIND EVERY SAVAGE, there's a story... We
don't just sell panties over here at SavagexFenty,
we represent the culture!

Twitter post, August 2, 2021

MEN, ESPECIALLY, THERE'S always a certain
figure that represents them in the space of
lingerie and loungewear and boxers and briefs.
It's always a six-pack or eight-pack. And we're
going to have men of all different sizes, all
different races. We're going to have men feel
included as well. Because I think that men have
been left behind in the inclusion curve that's
been happening.

Associated Press, September 22, 2021

I LOVE SEEING new faces and giving people an opportunity. Because, I mean, there's talent everywhere. When you see it you just gotta grab it.

on Savage X Fenty models, *Access Hollywood*,
September 22, 2021

WHEN I FOUND out I was pregnant, I thought to myself, There's no way I'm going to go shopping in no maternity aisle. I'm sorry—it's too much fun to get dressed up. I'm not going to let that part disappear because my body is changing.

Vogue, May 1, 2022

I'M HOPING THAT we were able to redefine what's considered "decent" for pregnant women. My body is doing incredible things right now, and I'm not going to be ashamed of that.

on her famous pregancy looks, *Vogue*, May 1, 2022

MY VISION HAD always been the celebration of the body and to continue to push the boundaries of what "sexy" meant, all built on the foundation of inclusivity.

Brand Disruptor Award acceptance speech at FEMMY Awards, August 2, 2022

DRESSING FOR PREGNANCY was such a piece of cake. But dressing in postpartum, what the f**k do you do? The week that I came home from the hospital—that was nothing but sweats and hoodies. But the weeks after that, you don't know what to put on.

British *Vogue*, February 15, 2023

I LIKE TO dress [my son] in things that don't look like baby clothes. I like to push it. I put him in floral stuff. I put him in hot pink. I love that. I think that fluidity in fashion is best.

British *Vogue*, February 15, 2023

Philanthropy and Activism

I DON'T THINK it's that people don't want to give. I just think that people want to know that they are making a difference when they give.

"Rihanna's Clara Lionel Foundation," June 19, 2015

IT'S AS SIMPLE as this: one day you could be the one. I mean, your kid, your kid's kids, your loved ones—nobody's exempt from disease and poverty.

"Rihanna's Clara Lionel Foundation," June 19, 2015

YOU KNOW, WHEN I started to experience the difference—or even have my race be highlighted—it was mostly when I would do business deals. And, you know, that never ends, by the way. It's still a thing. And it's the thing that makes me want to prove people wrong.

on having a different awareness of race after moving to the US, *T Magazine*, October 12, 2015

IF I CAN save one life, if I can give someone an extra day, an extra week, an extra year, an extra ten years, it's completely worth it.

**"Rihanna Gears Up for the Second Annual Diamond Ball Benefiting the Clara Lionel Foundation,"
December 7, 2015**

EVERY CHILD HAS something that they aspire to be.... Arts and culture might not literally be putting someone up on stage, but just giving them the outlet to do something that they might love. Keep them focused on positive things.

"Rihanna Shares Her Vision for the Clara Lionel Foundation," May 9, 2016

WOMEN FEEL EMPOWERED when they can do the things that are supposed to be only for men, you know? It breaks boundaries, it's liberating, and it's empowering when you feel like, Well, I can do that, too.

Vogue, April 1, 2016

YOU DON'T HAVE to be rich to help somebody. You don't have to be famous. You don't even have to be college educated.

2017 Harvard Humanitarian Award acceptance speech, February 28, 2017

TEACH YOUR KIDS love and equality. Teach them about the beauty in uniqueness and how to embrace others' differences!

Instagram post, December 11, 2017

THIS IS A fight that we're never going to stop fighting until every boy, and every girl, has access to education.

Global Partnership for Education conference, February 2, 2018

My grandmother always used to say: "If you've got a dollar, there's plenty to share."

2017 Harvard Humanitarian Award
acceptance speech, February 28, 2017

WE SUPPORT EVERYTHING from global education, to healthcare, emergency response programs all over the world. And it's going to keep spreading out because we don't see one person that we don't want to help.

on the Clara Lionel foundation, fourth annual Diamond Ball red carpet, September 13, 2018

CLARA AND LIONEL are both my grandparents who have both instilled in me the importance of giving back. So, to be able to raise funds for global education, health, and emergency response programs around the world at this magnitude is an ode to them and our greatest achievement.

fourth annual Diamond Ball, September 13, 2018

EDUCATION IS A lifelong journey. We never know everything, but we constantly evolve as we learn more about our communities, this ever-changing world and ourselves.

***The Guardian*, September 18, 2018**

IF WE CAN overcome the education deficit in the developing world, everybody wins.

The Guardian, September 18, 2018

YOUR BRAIN, YOUR mind, your knowledge, that's your own, and so that's your power. And I feel like everyone should have the opportunity to have access to that. It's a crime that people aren't having this access to education worldwide.

Studio 10, October 3, 2018

THERE'S NO GREATER responsibility than being in control of your future and the future starts NOW!!

Instagram post, October 9, 2018

IF YOU'RE TIRED of feeling like you don't matter in the political process, know the most important thing you can do in supporting a candidate is finding someone who will take on critical issues such as: making minimum wage a livable wage, paying teachers what [they're] worth, ensuring criminal justice reform, making healthcare a right, and repealing Stand Your Ground.

Instagram post, November 4, 2018

IF YOU'RE TIRED of complaining about the state of the country and government, get up and do something about it!!!

Instagram post, November 6, 2018

INTERNATIONAL WOMEN'S DAY errday… big ups to every beautiful spirit manifested as woman in this "man's" world!

Twitter post, March 8, 2019

#INCLUSIVITY that's what I stand for.

Instagram post, May 1, 2019

YOU DESERVE TO be treated with the highest level of respect today and every day for your selfless thankless role in our lives. Here's to the women who raise us, teach us, feed us, nurture us, mold us, discipline us, and love us unconditionally!

Instagram post on Mother's Day, May 12, 2019

I WILL *NOT* back down from being a woman, from being black, from having an opinion. I'm running a company and that's exactly what I came here to do. I don't know if it makes people uncomfortable or not, but that's not even my business, you know? I *do* know that the reason I'm here is not *because* I'm black. It's because of what I have to offer.

T Magazine, May 19, 2019

I PRAY FOR the safety of the Sudanese people.
They have a right to speak out and demand
peace, justice, and a transition to civilian rule....
Military rulers need to be held accountable.

Instagram post, June 30, 2019

IMAGINE A WORLD where it's easier to get an
AK-47 than a VISA! Imagine a world where they
build a wall to keep terrorists IN AMERICA!!!...
Nobody deserves to die like this. NOBODY!

in response to the mass shooting in El Paso, Texas,
Instagram post, August 4, 2019

I CAN BELIEVE in something, but I cannot make
anyone believe in that. And for them to give
their heart, their gifts, their life, their day, their
time, their donations—it means a lot and it's
something that cannot go unacknowledged.

on attendees and performers who participate in the
Diamond Ball, fifth annual Diamond Ball red carpet,
September 13, 2019

I DO A lot of things that are of creative outlets. . . .
But there's nothing more important than saving
lives, helping lives, and making lives better.
And this is the most important thing that I do
in my life.

fifth annual Diamond Ball red carpet,
September 12, 2019

I FEEL LIKE the darkness has actually forced
people to find this light within them where
they want to do better. It's easy when you think
everything is going really well and perfect. When
everything is flowers and butterflies and you're
in your own bubble and your own world. But to
see it, to know it's happening—it pushes you to
want to be the light in the world.

Vogue, **November 1, 2019**

I<small>F THERE IS</small> anything that I've learned, [it's] that we can only fix this world together. We can't do it divided. I cannot emphasize that enough. We can't let the desensitivity seep in. The "If it's your problem, then it's not mine." "It's a woman's problem." "It's a Black people problem." "It's a poor people problem."

President's Award acceptance speech at NAACP Image Awards, February 22, 2020

W<small>HEN I SEE</small> these injustices happening, it's hard to turn a blind eye. It's hard to pretend it's not happening. The things that I refuse to stay silent on, these are things that I genuinely believe in.

British *Vogue*, May 1, 2020

I<small>F INTENTIONAL</small> MURDER is the fit consequence for "drugs" or "resisting arrest"….then what's the fit consequence for MURDER???! #GeorgeFloyd #AhmaudArbery #BreonnaTaylor

Twitter post, May 29, 2020

FOR THE LAST few days, the magnitude of devastation, anger, sadness I've felt has been overwhelming to say the least! Watching my people get murdered and lynched day after day pushed me to a heavy place in my heart!

**in response to the murder of George Floyd,
Instagram post, May 29, 2020**

VOTE. YA AIN'T got shit else to do man! Get yo ass off the couch and go vote!!! I don't wanna hear another excuse!! Stop believing that your vote and voice don't matter! This the illest way to protest...vote for the change you want!!!

Twitter post, June 2, 2020

WHAT HAPPENED YESTERDAY in Atlanta was brutal, tragic, and is certainly not an isolated incident by any means. AAPI hate has been rampantly perpetuated and it's disgusting! I'm heartbroken for the Asian community and my heart is with the loved ones of those we lost yesterday. The hate must stop.

in response to the 2021 racially-motivated spa shootings in Atlanta, Instagram post, March 17, 2021

WE ARE AND will continue to be relentless in our pursuit to shift inaction to action, oppression to agency, injustice to justice.

Clara Lionel Foundation 2020 Annual Report, June 23, 2021

EVERY DOLLAR I make, I want to give it back. When it comes to people who need help, it hurts when I can't do as much as I want, so now we're just putting our foot down and [the Clara Lionel Foundation] is about to grow in a way that I'm really proud of.

***New York Times*, September 23, 2021**

Milestones

1988

- Robyn Rihanna Fenty is born on February 20, 1988, in the Parish of St. Michael, one of 11 parishes, or regions, of Barbados. She is the first of three children born to Monica Braithwaite and Ronald Fenty. Monica is of Guyanese origin and an accountant. Ronald, a Barbadian, works as a warehouse supervisor.

- Raised in Bridgetown, the capital city of Barbados, Robyn's childhood and early teenage years are fraught with domestic and personal troubles. Ronald struggles with alcoholism and addiction and is physically abusive at home. Robyn suffers from debilitating headaches during this period. She seeks the help of doctors, but they have trouble pinpointing the cause of the problem. At school she is shy and a bit of a loner, and her classmates bully her for having lighter skin than them. She finds solace in music and listens avidly to pop divas and reggae.

2002

- After years of marital instability and periods of separation, Monica and Ronald divorce. Robyn is 14 and her headaches have begun to subside. She forms a singing group with two of her high school classmates as an outlet for her passion for music.

2003

- Robyn and her groupmates audition for American record producer Evan Rogers while he vacations in Barbados with his wife, who is from there. Robyn sings a Destiny's Child cover and outshines her companions in Rogers's eyes. He invites her to a meeting the next day, along with her mother, to discuss next steps for a potential career in music. For the next year she travels on and off to the U.S. to work with Rogers on a demo tape.

2004

- Robyn relocates from Barbados to the U.S. and arranges to stay with Rogers and his wife in Connecticut. She signs a deal with Syndicated Rhythm Productions, the production company belonging to Rogers and his partner Carl Sturken. They send her demo tape to record labels.

2005

- Def Jam Recordings expresses interest in Robyn's demo and invites her to audition for the label. She performs her demo track "Pon de Replay," with choreography, for renowned rapper and company president Jay-Z, and for CEO L.A. Reid. Reid is so impressed that he asks her not to leave the building until they have worked out a contract. She remains in the office until 3 a.m. and signs her first record deal.

- Her debut single, "Pon de Replay," comes out to generally positive reviews and finds success on domestic and international music charts, peaking at number two on the *Billboard* Hot 100. The track is released under her stage name: Rihanna.

- Rihanna's debut studio album, *Music of the Sun,* hits the shelves later that year. It's received by critics with mixed reviews but experiences modest commercial success in its first six months, earning a gold certification from the Recording Industry Association of America (RIAA) for 500,000 units shipped or sold.

2006

- *A Girl Like Me*, her second studio album, is released to the public. It is her first album to become certified platinum, selling one million units within four months of its debut. The song "SOS" rises to the top of the U.S. *Billboard* Hot 100 and is Rihanna's first single to chart there at number one. Reviews of *A Girl Like Me* are generally more favorable than those of *Music of the Sun,* but still fall short of a critical consensus.

- This year also marks Rihanna's first appearance in a feature film, with a brief cameo role as herself in the cheerleader comedy *Bring It On: All or Nothing*.

2007

- Rihanna's third album, *Good Girl Gone Bad,* is a critical success and marks a breakthrough year in her career. It also represents a new, bold shift in her artistic sound and style. While her music moves past the Caribbean vibes of her last two records and into edgier, up-tempo dance-pop productions, her image as

the innocent island girl gives way to a confident woman
with shorter hair, more attitude, and greater sex appeal.
The album garners four Grammy nominations and a
win in the Best Rap/Sung Collaboration category for
the song "Umbrella," which features Jay-Z. "Umbrella"
is a massive commercial success and tops the charts in
a dozen countries for weeks on end. Rihanna launches
her first worldwide tour to promote the album.

2009

- Rihanna is scheduled to perform at the 51st Annual
  Grammy Awards, but abruptly cancels on the day of the
  ceremony. Reports surface that her boyfriend, singer
  Chris Brown, has turned himself in to the L.A. Police
  and been arrested for assault. It's later revealed that
  Rihanna has been victim to physical abuse at his hands.
  Photographs leaked from a police station show her face
  bruised and swollen, injuries sustained when Brown
  turned violent as the couple argued on their return
  from a party the night before the Grammys. Faced with
  unrelenting questions and opinions from the media,
  she remains silent on the incident for much of the year,
  but eventually speaks about it to Diane Sawyer in an
  interview on *20/20*.

- Reports surface of Rihanna at work in the studio soon
  after the incident with Brown. *Rated R* comes out
  later that year. Her fourth studio album—as its title
  suggests—is more intense and provocative than her
  previous work. It's well-reviewed by critics and leads
  some to speculate that the singer's personal and public
  hardships that year may have fed the fire of creativity
  and artistic growth.

2010

- Rihanna wins her second and third Grammys for the song "Run this Town," alongside Jay-Z and Kanye West. She takes home awards for Best Rap/Sung Collaboration and Best Rap Song.

- She and Jay-Z unite again to support humanitarian aid for Haiti in the wake of a devastating earthquake there, joining Bono and The Edge to record the song "Stranded (Haiti Mon Amour)" as part of the *Hope for Haiti No*w campaign. She also appears on Kanye's album *My Beautiful Dark Twisted Fantasy* later that year. "Love the Way You Lie," a collaboration between Rihanna and Eminem, is an international chart-topping mega-hit.

- Her fifth studio album, *Loud*, is released in November. It includes a second Eminem collaboration—"Love the Way You Lie (Part II)"—and guest appearances by Nicki Minaj and Drake. It also brings the hit songs "What's My Name" and "Only Girl (In the World)," which both hit number one on the *Billboard* Hot 100. The album is received favorably by critics, if less enthusiastically than her previous couple of releases. Reviewers note a return to the brighter, more upbeat style of music that preceded *Rated R*.

2011

- The perfume Reb'l Fleur is released for sale, becoming Rihanna's debut fragrance and marking her first foray into the perfume and cosmetics industry. The name is based on a term of endearment from her grandmother, who would call her "Rebel Flower."

- She also makes inroads into the fashion industry this year, teaming up with Italian fashion house Armani to create her first fashion collection. She designs jeans, jackets, T-shirts, and lingerie for the company's Emporio Armani Underwear and Armani Jeans lines.

- The song "Only Girl (In the World)," off of last year's *Loud*, wins Rihanna her fourth Grammy. The award is for Best Dance Recording and is her first win for a solo track.

- Rihanna secures 18 *Billboard* Music Award nominations, more than any other artist that year. She wins Top Rap Song for "Love the Way You Lie," as well as Top Female Artist and Top Radio Songs Artist.

- Rihanna's sixth studio album, *Talk That Talk,* is released in November. Reviews are generally positive, even if they fail again to overshadow the critical consensus on her work of several years' past. The track "We Found Love," which features Calvin Harris, is a smash hit across the globe and earns Rihanna her longest ever consecutive number one spot on the *Billboard* Hot 100 chart.

2012

- The pop star wins her fifth Grammy for "All of the Lights," a collaboration with Kanye West, Kid Cudi, and Fergie. It's the third time that she wins in the category Best Rap/Sung Collaboration.

- *TIME* names Rihanna one of The World's 100 Most Influential People.

- The movie *Battleship* comes out in May and features Rihanna in her first major film role. She plays a weapons specialist in the military's fight against an invading alien force. While the film is a commercial and critical flop, the novice actress receives encouraging feedback on her performance.

- Clara Braithwaite, Rihanna's maternal grandmother—affectionately known to her as Gran Gran Dolly—dies of cancer. Rihanna founds the Clara Lionel Foundation (CLF) later that year in honor of her late grandmother and surviving grandfather, Lionel. Her first act of charity through CLF is to donate modern radiotherapy equipment to the Queen Elizabeth Hospital in Barbados. In the years that follow, the foundation expands its reach by raising funds for disaster relief, climate resilience, and global education initiatives.

- The British reality show *Styled to Rock* premieres, with Rihanna as its executive producer and host. In the series, contestants are mentored by Rihanna and other fashion and entertainment professionals while competing to create the winning outfit for a different celebrity musician each week. The final two competitors go head-to-head to design something for Rihanna herself, who goes on to wear the winning outfit for her performance at the Wireless Festival in London. Rihanna also executive produces the American version of the show, which comes out the following year and includes Miley Cyrus and Carly Rae Jepsen as guest judges, among others.

- Rihanna embarks on her 777 Tour, so-named because it consists of seven concert performances in seven different countries within seven days and is meant to promote the upcoming release of her seventh album. She charters a plane for the journey and invites approximately 150 journalists from 82 countries to accompany her, as well as some fans and a film crew. A documentary on the tour, titled *Rihanna 777*, is eventually released, though it glosses over the problems that many invitees experienced, such as little-to-no contact with the singer herself and grueling stretches of time on planes and buses waiting for her to return.

- *Unapologetic*, Rihanna's seventh studio album, is released to mixed reviews. Despite its critical shortcomings, the work boasts several unprecedented successes for the singer. It debuts as number one on the *Billboard* 200 chart—her first such album to do so—and sells more copies in its first week than any of her previous releases. Its lead single, "Diamonds," charts at number one on the *Billboard* Hot 100.

2013

- Rihanna strikes up a fashion partnership—her second, following Armani—with English clothing brand River Island. She is granted creative liberty to design several seasonal collections. Her first—a Spring/Summer collection—premiers at London Fashion Week. Her Autumn/Winter collection is released later that year.

- For the music video to her 2011 hit "We Found Love," Rihanna wins the Grammy Award for Best Short Form Music Video—her first in that category and sixth overall.

- Cosmetics company MAC announces they've signed Rihanna for a collaboration on several seasonal collections. The product line—RiRi Hearts MAC—is introduced with a red "RiRi Woo" lipstick and grows to include eye and face makeup products, nail polish, and accessories. It marks her first creative endeavor in the beauty industry.

- At the *Billboard* Music Awards, she takes home the prize for Top R&B Album (*Unapologetic*) and Top R&B Song ("Diamonds"). They are her first *Billboard* wins for an album and for a solo track.

- She makes a cameo appearance as herself in the apocalyptic comedy film *This Is the End*.

2014

- *Unapologetic* wins Best Urban Contemporary Album at the Grammys, giving Rihanna her seventh award from the Recording Academy in seven years.

- After nine years and seven albums with Def Jam Recordings, Rihanna departs from the company and signs with Roc Nation, the record label founded by Jay-Z in 2009. The deal represents a strengthening of ties between Rihanna and Roc Nation, which has managed her career since 2010.

- The Council of Fashion Designers of America (CFDA) bestows its Fashion Icon Award on Rihanna at its annual fashion awards. She famously attends the event in a see-through dress that's studded with Swarovski crystals. Her regret from that night, she later admits, is not that she didn't wear a bra, but that she didn't bedazzle her thong.

- Rihanna hosts her inaugural Diamond Ball, a charity event in support of her Clara Lionel Foundation and its global education, health, and emergency initiatives. After an introduction from Brad Pitt, she takes to the stage in a gown and performs her music, with orchestral accompaniment, to a crowd of celebrities. The gala becomes CLF's signature annual event and is hosted at different locations following its initial success in Beverly Hills.

- German sportswear manufacturer Puma enlists Rihanna as their creative director of women's apparel. The first brainchild of the partnership—the Puma Creeper sneaker—is a massive success. The shoe sells out within three hours of its release and goes on to win Shoe of the Year at the *Footwear News* Achievement Awards.

- She makes a brief cameo appearance in the movie musical *Annie*. Her character has only a couple lines, but it suggests that her interest in acting continues unabated.

2015

- Rihanna receives her eighth Grammy for her collaboration with Eminem on his 2013 song "The Monster." It's her fourth win for Best Rap/Sung Collaboration.

- In her animated film debut, for the movie *Home*, she voices Tip, a teenager who befriends an alien visiting earth. Jim Parsons, Steven Martin, and Jennifer Lopez star alongside her in the sci-fi comedy. Rihanna's performance wins her Outstanding Voice Performance at the Black Reel Awards and a nomination for Favorite Animated Movie Voice at the People's Choice Awards. She also records three songs for the movie's original motion picture soundtrack, making her the only artist with more than a single track on the eight-song release.

- Rihanna steals the show at the Met Gala's red carpet. She arrives in a fur-lined, ornately embroidered yellow gown attached to a commanding 16-foot train. The dress is made by Chinese fashion designer Guo Pei and weighs 50 pounds. The iconic ensemble enhances Rihanna's reputation for bold, boundary-breaking fashion.

- French fashion house Dior recruits Rihanna as their brand ambassador, making her the first Black woman to hold the position. She films with the company in Versailles as part of their Secret Garden campaign.

- The pop star makes music history when she surpasses 100 million gold and platinum song certifications. She is the first recording artist in the history of the RIAA to reach such a milestone.

- Rihanna is named contributing creative director of Stance—an American sock, underwear, and apparel manufacturer—as well as one of the company's brand ambassadors. In her creative role, she helps design sock collections for Stance's women's division. An early, limited-edition release to commemorate the partnership is called "Murder Rih Wrote" and consists of crew and over-the-knee socks with collage-style prints of graphics and text in white, black, and red. Later collaborations come out under the name "Fenty x Stance" and incorporate details like bows and lace. The "Iconic Looks" collection renders Rihanna as a knitted figure, dressed in some of her most memorable outfits, down the length of the socks.

2016

- After months of delays and an accidental leak, Rihanna's eighth studio album, *Anti*, is released. At the time, it concludes the longest wait between albums of the singer's career, with more than three years having elapsed since 2012's *Unapologetic*. *Anti* garners ample praise and is viewed by many critics as her best work to date. While the release is also not without its detractors, both camps note its shift towards experimentation and away from the dance-pop tendencies that have characterized so much of her music in the past. *Anti* brings the hit song "Work," which features Drake and charts at number one on the *Billboard* Hot 100 for nine weeks. It comes as a surprise to many that three of Rihanna's hit singles from the previous year—"FourFiveSeconds" (featuring Kanye West and Paul McCartney), "Bitch

Better Have My Money," and "American Oxygen"—fail to make it onto the album.

- Rihanna makes inroads into luxury fashion by partnering with renowned Spanish fashion designer Manolo Blahnik. Their collection, "Denim Desserts," makes elaborate use of denim fabric, jewels, sequins, and embroidery. The footwear is carried exclusively in New York, London, and Hong Kong, and retails between $900 and $4,000.

- Her Dior brand ambassadorship yields a hands-on collaboration with the luxury line. She helps design a collection of futuristic sunglasses inspired by the character Geordi La Forge from *Star Trek*. The "Rihanna" collection, as it's simply known, marks the first time that the house's ambassador is given creative authority in a company collaboration.

2017

- Harvard University names Rihanna Humanitarian of the Year, citing the contributions of her Clara Lionel Foundation to medical facilities in Barbados, as well as its work in providing access to education for girls in developing countries. In her acceptance speech for the Peter J. Gomes Humanitarian Award, she asserts that to be a humanitarian "all you need to do is help one person, expecting nothing in return."

- Rihanna makes her television acting debut in the final season of *Bates Motel*, a modern-day prequel to Alfred Hitchcock's psychological thriller *Psycho*. She plays Marion Crane, the iconic character from the famous "shower scene" in the 1960 film, in a performance that's fairly well-reviewed. The producers admit that they sought Rihanna for the role after reading a profile of hers in *Vanity Fair*, where she confessed that *Bates Motel* was her favorite show.

- Rihanna tests her design skills in a new field by working with Swiss luxury jeweler Chopard—a brand she's partial to and has worn on numerous red carpets over the years—on a jewelry collection. The fruit of their collaboration is the "Rihanna Loves Chopard" collection, which features highly ornate, brightly jeweled, Barbados-inspired pieces, as well as more minimalistic creations composed of jungle-green ceramic and gold. The collection launches at the 70th annual Cannes Film Festival in France.

- She appears in a minor role in the science fiction film *Valerian and the City of a Thousand Planets*. Her character puts on an elaborate dance routine as a shape-shifting, far-future cabaret performer.

- Rihanna launches Fenty Beauty in more than a dozen countries. The beauty brand—a joint business venture between Rihanna and French luxury goods giant Moët Hennessy Louis Vuitton (LVMH)—is a massive success, bringing in $100 million in its first month and $550 million its first year. It earns a reputation for inclusivity and distinguishes itself from other brands by offering 40 shades of foundation at the outset. The number of shades and range of skin tones is so unprecedented in the industry that other cosmetics companies—in what comes to be known as "The Fenty Effect"—follow suit and begin to increase the number of shades they offer. *TIME* magazine honors Fenty Beauty as one of the 25 best inventions of the year.

2018

- For her collaboration with Kendrick Lamar on his song "Loyalty," Rihanna wins the ninth Grammy of her career. The award is for Best Rap/Sung Performance.

- Rihanna is named to the *TIME* 100 Most Influential People for a second time. She's labelled an "icon," one of five categories added to the magazine's annual honor since she last made the list in 2012 (the other four being "pioneers," "artists," "leaders," and "titans").

- Rihanna launches her lingerie brand Savage X Fenty online. The company is launched in partnership with TechStyle Fashion Group and becomes Rihanna's second business in the "Fenty" brand family. It consists of lingerie and sleepwear and, true to its sister brand, emphasizes inclusivity in its diverse offering of sizes and shades of nude. The line is such a hit that its entire inventory is gone within a month.

- Rihanna plays a hacker in the heist film *Ocean's 8*, joining an ensemble female cast that includes Sandra Bullock, Cate Blanchett, and Anne Hathaway.

- The Barbadian government names Rihanna "Ambassador Extraordinary and Plenipotentiary" of her native country. The role involves promoting the educational, touristic, and financial well-being of the island.

2019

- *Guava Island*, a musical romance, is released on Amazon Prime Video. Rihanna plays the film's central love interest, alongside leading man Donald Glover.

- Rihanna launches Fenty, a luxury fashion line, in partnership with LVMH. It marks not only the first new brand that LVMH has built since 1987, but also the first time that a Black woman has led a major luxury fashion label for the French conglomerate. The brand first displays its wares at a pop-up store in Paris before moving online.

- The first Savage X Fenty Show premiers on Amazon Prime Video. It combines runway fashion-show elements with choreographed dances and performances by high-profile musicians. Rihanna, who serves as the show's creative director and executive producer, describes it as a "fashion musical" that highlights people and characteristics not typically associated with the world of fashion or society's commonplace conceptions of "sexy." The show is well-received and praised for its diversity, leading to new annual shows in subsequent years.

- Rihanna publishes her self-titled coffee table book, *Rihanna*. The book, which is dubbed a "visual autobiography," has been five years in the making, is 500 pages long, and retails for $150. It contains over 1,000 color photographs of Rihanna throughout her career, many of them taken by and some of them featuring Melissa Forde, her longtime best friend. Some signed limited editions of the book are also released to the tune of $5,500. Cardi B famously pays $111,000 as the winning bid for an exclusive signed copy at Rihanna's fifth annual Diamond Ball.

2020

- Rihanna receives the President's Award at the NAACP Image Awards. It is given annually "in recognition of special achievement and distinguished public service." The organization cites her accomplishments as an artist, entrepreneur, philanthropist, activist, as well as her charitable work, in their choice to grant her the prestigious honor.

- Fenty Skin—a skin care line—becomes the newest addition to Rihanna's Fenty empire. The brand is released with a modest line of three items—cleanser, toner, and sunscreen—which are intended to complement Fenty Beauty products. It later expands to include more face and body care products, such as an eye cream, lip mask, and moisturizer.

2021

- LVMH announces that the Fenty clothing line will be discontinued. Observers note that supply chain shortages and declines in luxury sales during the COVID-19 pandemic may have factored into the company's decision.

- *Forbes* declares Rihanna a billionaire. The company estimates her net worth at $1.7 billion, owing mostly to her 50 percent stake in Fenty Beauty. This makes her the wealthiest female musician and second wealthiest female entertainer on the planet.

- Rihanna is declared a National Hero of Barbados, earning her the honorific "The Right Honorable Robyn Rihanna Fenty" and adding her to the ranks of only 10 other Barbadians to be granted the title. She receives the honor at the same ceremony in which the island nation renounces its status as a colony of Great Britain and inaugurates their first ever president.

2022

- *Vogue* features a pregnant Rihanna wearing a bright red lace bodysuit on the cover of its May issue. Her third-trimester baby bump is also on conspicuous display in a series of instantly iconic photographs within the magazine, as well as in social media posts from Rihanna herself. The bold fashion statement is in keeping with Rihanna's reluctance to wear conventional maternity clothes while carrying the child, and an explicit attempt, according to her, "to redefine what's considered 'decent' for pregnant women."

- Rihanna gives birth to her first child, a boy, alongside her partner A$AP Rocky. The child's name is not immediately revealed to the public.

- The song "Lift Me Up" is released as the lead single for the soundtrack to the movie *Black Panther: Wakanda Forever*. It is Rihanna's first solo musical recording to come out since *Anti* came out more than six years prior. The soundtrack includes a second song by Rihanna ("Born Again"), but it is "Lift Me Up" that later earns her an Oscar nomination for Best Original Song—the first Oscar nomination of her career.

2023

- Rihanna headlines the Super Bowl LVII halftime show—her first live performance in five years. She previously turned down the 2019 halftime show, citing the NFL's treatment of Colin Kaepernick. Although initially unsure about taking on the 2023 halftime show, which is now produced by Jay-Z's Roc Nation, she commits to the challenge as a way to celebrate all of her music and get back on stage, saying it's "now or never." This point becomes even more clear when she performs her setlist of 12 hit songs on a floating platform above a sea of dancers—all while showing off a baby bump. Immediately afterwards, her representatives confirm that she is pregnant with her second child, making the performance yet another example of Rihanna pushing the boundaries of how a pregnant woman should look.

Acknowledgments

We would like to thank Emily Feng, Amanda Gibson, Paige Gilberg, Eva Lopez, Hannah Manion, Grace Mathew, Yola Mzizi, Suzanne Sonnier, Mira Green, and Joy Zhao for their invaluable contributions to the preparation of this manuscript.

MORE FROM AGATE'S BESTSELLING IN THEIR OWN WORDS SERIES

Thought-provoking, inspiring quotations from some of the world's most illuminating leaders and cultural icons

RuPaul
In His Own Words
$12.95 | 978-1-57284-279-3

Martha Stewart
In Her Own Words
$12.95 |978-1-57284-288-5

Taylor Swift
In Her Own Words
$12.95 | 978-1-57284-278-6

AND MORE...

Jeff Bezos:
In His Own Words
978-1-57284-265-6

Ruth Bader Ginsberg:
In Her Own Words
978-1-57284-249-6

Dolly Parton: In Her Own
Words
978-1-57284-294-6

Bill Gates: In His Own
Words
978-1-57284-292-2

Michelle Obama: In Her
Own Words
978-1-57284-295-3

Elon Musk: In His Own
Words
978-1-57284-298-4

Oprah Winfrey In Her Own
Words
978-1-57284-322-6

Jane Fonda In Her Own
Words
978-1-57284-302-8